Managing Change in Higher Education

SRHE *and Open University Press Imprint*
General Editor: Heather Eggins

Managing Change in Higher Education

A Learning Environment Architecture

Peter Ford
Peter Goodyear
Richard Heseltine
Roger Lewis
Jonathan Darby
Joyce Graves
Pat Sartorius
Dave Harwood
Tom King

Society for Research into Higher Education
& Open University Press

Published by SRHE and
Open University Press
Celtic Court
22 Ballmoor
Buckingham
MK18 1XW

and 1900 Frost Road, Suite 101
Bristol, PA 19007, USA

First published 1996

A catalogue record of this book is available from the British Library

ISBN 0 335 19791 4 (pb)   0 335 19792 2 (hb)

Library of Congress Cataloging-in-Publication Data

Managing change in higher education: a learning environment
   architecture / Peter Ford . . . [et al.].
      p.   cm.
   Includes bibliographical references and index.
   ISBN 0-335-19792-2.—ISBN 0-335-19791-4 (pbk.)
   1. Education. Higher—Great Britain—Administration.
   2. Universities and colleges—Great Britain—Business management.
   3. Education, Higher—Aims and objectives—Great Britain
   4. Educational planning—Great Britain.   I. Ford, Peter. Professor.
   LB2341.8.G7M36   1996
   378.1'01—dc20   96-28690
                                                                            CIP

Editing and production coordination by
The Running Head Limited, London and Cambridge
Typeset by Type Study, Scarborough
Printed in Great Britain by St Edmundsbury Press
Bury St Edmunds, Suffolk

Contents

Notes on the Authors

Professor Peter Ford is Dean of Science at the University of Nottingham.

Professor Peter Goodyear is head of the Department of Educational Research at the University of Lancaster.

Dr Richard Heseltine is Director of Academic Services and Librarian at the University of Hull.

Professor Roger Lewis is BP Professor of Learning Development, University of Humberside.

Jonathan Darby is Director of Technology-assisted Lifelong Learning at the University of Oxford.

Joyce Graves is Head of Applications Support at the University of Nottingham.

Pat Sartorius is Learning Technologies Consultant at Peritas Limited.

Dave Harwood is a Systems Architect at ICL, Enterprise Technology.

Tom King is a Development Manager at ICL, Lifelong Learning.

Foreword

Higher education institutions are immensely rich and complex environments. Much of that richness and complexity has arisen, over the years, from their ready acceptance of certain kinds of change: change as it affects the development of disciplinary and interdisciplinary paradigms; change as individuals and groups absorb and reflect upon new discoveries; and change as the academic community responds to its host society.

Other types of change have proved more difficult: enlarging both the number and the diversity of external clients; dealing with new assumptions about the economy of the system; and, above all, internal organisational change and its management. For many within the university or college, the notion of 'managing' rather than simply 'administering' these things remains anathema.

It is a distinct virtue of the 'learning architecture' project that it has faced these tensions head-on and in a holistic manner. The result is a powerful conceptualisation of the academic process, its physical and economic environment, and the techniques of constructive change. It is also deeply respectful of both the continuing and changing objectives of the higher education enterprise. As such it offers a practical and flexible contribution to the achievement of a difficult task.

Professor David Watson
Director of the University of Brighton

Preface

Readership

The authors hope that this book will appeal to a broad readership of all those in the UK higher education sector who are involved in the delivery of student learning. In this we would include:

- Vice-chancellors and principals along with the others in the senior management team
- Those who are directly involved in teaching and learning support in its many forms
- Those who provide the wider set of services to support the student learning process, such as librarians and computer specialists.

We also hope that the book will be of value to the external stakeholders such as government, industrial partners and suppliers, and that the principles of the approach will be appreciated by readers in other UK education sectors, not to mention any overseas readers.

How to use this book

We hope that as our readers accept and start to consider how to implement the methodology described, that they will find the book a useful point of reference for guidance. Depending on individual areas of interest, readers will no doubt wish to look more in depth at different sections after they have considered the principles we introduce.

However, rather than pointing particular readers at particular chapters to begin with, we would recommend that each reader first reads through the book as a whole. The chapters do become progressively more detailed and we anticipate that some sections in some chapters will be skimmed at first reading.

The book tends to be focused on a whole-institution approach but we would recommend that deans, heads of schools and departments, and others, should consider the applicability of the method to their own domains as well as from an institutional perspective.

Further reading

Appendix A, Bibliography, contains a list of the other books available in the OPEN*framework* series and additional reading material.

Trademarks

OPEN*framework* is a trademark of International Computers Limited. UNIX is a registered trademark of X/Open Company Limited. Windows and Windows NT are registered trademarks of Microsoft Corporation.

Acknowledgements

The authors would like to acknowledge their grateful thanks to all those who responded to their request to comment on a draft version of this book. The inputs received were very welcome and did have an influence on the final presentation before publication. Respondents may well recognise some of their own words now reflected in certain sections.

1

Introduction

Building a higher education system for the next generation

All providers of higher education today are faced with the challenge of building a system of higher education which will be equipped to meet the needs of society in the next century. The requirement to respond positively to change and to manage it effectively has never been so urgent. Universities, and other institutions which provide higher education (HEIs), are now subject to an unprecedented level of external scrutiny; the demands made of them have expanded, and expectations have changed. HEIs inhabit a more competitive world, where resources have become scarcer and where the impact of technology has never been so great or so unpredictable. They have entered global educational markets, while also forging local and regional links which are blurring the distinctions between study and employment and between different sectors of educational provision.

These themes of transformation and renewal are nowhere more apparent than in the context of teaching and learning. From one point of view, this is primarily a question of numbers. Within a relatively short period of time, we have moved from an elite to a mass system of higher education, and despite the present phase of consolidation of student numbers, there is every reason to think that there will be renewed expansion. But more profound changes are taking place, changes which seem likely to alter the very nature of higher education.

Already the profile of the student population has been transformed. The channels of access to higher education have been broadened and multiplied. For the first time we have more students over the age of 21 than under it. We have more and more part-time students. The expectations and learning styles of these students are increasingly diverse. Learning itself is now regarded as a lifelong activity, not something sandwiched between childhood and work. Distance learning is becoming commonplace, in terms of both global and local provision, and systems are being put in place to credit students for prior experience and learning, thus freeing them to move from one institution to another and to construct qualifications from multiple institutional sources.

Encouraged by the needs articulated by employers, there is increasing emphasis on providing students with lifelong skills, less on subject content.

These are massive changes, and there is growing recognition that they cannot be sustained on the basis of traditional models of teaching and learning alone. It is clear that if HEIs are going to adapt successfully to very different circumstances, and respond effectively to the changed expectations of students, employers and society as a whole, then it will be necessary to rethink the ways in which teaching and learning are supported.

The Learning Environment Architecture

The *Learning Environment Architecture* provides a method for developing and managing learning environments to support the current and changing role of higher education in the United Kingdom. It does this by providing a method for creating a framework within which strategies, business processes and supporting information systems can be developed and changed to meet the objectives of an institution with maximum overall effectiveness.

In the context of this book, an architecture is defined as a framework aligning the needs of the business, its people and the capabilities of technology which recognises that they are all continuously changing. It is a tool which provides a structure for managing this change and a set of standards, conventions and rules which support the effective integration of business, social and technical systems. *It provides a method for managing change.*

The Learning Environment Architecture is a method which assists a learning institution in creating, implementing and monitoring its own learning environment.

What makes the Learning Environment Architecture different from other methods is that:

- It is specific to learning environments
- It is based on the principle that diversity and change are forces to be managed and harnessed rather than resisted
- It flows from business through to information systems so that all systems and processes clearly support the aims of the learning institution
- It incorporates a value system
- It is supplier-independent, which means it accommodates any supplier's products
- The resulting architecture is designed to cope with changes which will occur in the future, for although not all changes can be foreseen, the architecture can be used to control specific events such as planning a new organisational structure, redefining a strategy or establishing a procurement policy.

Scope

This Learning Environment Architecture focuses on learning environments in UK higher education. It provides a generic model which can be used by

any individual learning institution to develop a learning environment architecture of their own. It is hoped that other education sectors in the UK –
further, secondary and primary – will also find it useful should they wish to
start developing such models for themselves.

The Learning Environment Architecture is based on the principles of
OPEN*framework*, which is described later in this chapter. It uses the business
and technical analysis methods provided by OPEN*framework* to create this specialised architecture for UK higher education.

Benefits

A learning institution using the Learning Environment Architecture to create
its own architecture can expect a number of benefits:

- A forward vision for the institution
- A common understanding
- Better internal collaboration
- A clear projection of purpose to the outside world
- A means of managing change in a fast-moving environment, by using the
  architecture as an anchor when all around is undergoing change
- The establishment of a quality learning environment
- Cost savings by:
  - aligning the organisational structure and business processes to the aims
    of the institution
  - using a consistent approach at both institutional and departmental levels
  - adopting an evolutionary approach which incorporates existing assets
    and systems
  - managing the effective introduction of new learning methods and sup-
    porting services
  - adopting a supplier-independent approach, avoiding tie-ins to particular
    suppliers
- Information systems which:
  - improve efficiency through a high degree of usability, helping staff and
    students to carry out their functions more effectively
  - are clearly aligned to the learning environment's direction and require-
    ments, and are flexible enough to accommodate future changes in both
    the learning environment's strategy and future developments in tech-
    nology.

OPEN*framework* approach

Rapid changes both in the information technology industry and in business
generally mean that enterprises, such as HEIs, must engage in a continuous
realignment of their business and technical systems.

OPEN*framework* is a method for managing change which aligns these
systems using the principles of architecture. It reduces the intrinsic

complexity by describing all aspects of an enterprise using three simple concepts:

* Perspectives
* Qualities
* Elements.

Perspectives are views of the enterprise from different sets of people, both inside and outside the enterprise. Different perspectives are used for the business and technical systems. Views are expressed as a set of issues and needs. For example, a manager perspective is likely to include cost and quality issues, whereas a trading partner perspective would include the ease of doing business with the institution, and a developer perspective might include the need for specialist development tools.

Qualities provide a value system. They are a set of yardsticks used to measure the different aspects of the institution's business, social and technical systems, in terms everyone involved can clearly understand. These systems form the core of the architecture and are described as you proceed through the book. The qualities are used to set specific goals for where you want the institution to get to, at a defined time in the future.

For example, a business performance goal might set a target for a certain percentage of students to be learning off-campus by a specific date. A social system performance goal might specify the throughput of the key business processes and the output that different people produce. An information system performance goal might specify a system work rate or an acceptable range for responsiveness. These are all examples of the performance quality.

Five qualities have been chosen which are simple to use, yet comprehensive in their scope: availability, usability, performance, security and potential for change. These are discussed further in Chapter 4.

Elements are used to describe the parts of a system. Different elements are used for business, social and technical systems.

As you read through the book you will come across some new terms which are specific to the method in terms of a learning environment. Terms such as *learnplace* and *learning chunk*. We have developed these terms because we believe that they describe objects which require a particular definition in the context of the method; we wanted to ensure that we did not use terminology similar to that already in everyday use, as we felt this would lead to unnecessary confusion. These terms are defined in full at the most appropriate point in the text and are also included in the Glossary, Appendix B.

If you wish to pursue topics in more detail, a list of further reading is given in Appendix A.

The method

The method presented in this book specialises the generic OPEN*framework* method to meet the requirements of learning environments for higher education institutions in the United Kingdom.

The method for developing architecture for an institution is shown in Figure 1.1.

The circular arrow to the right of the diagram is there to indicate that the method is a continuous, repetitive process and that the development of an architecture is not intended to be a one-off exercise to address only the change requirements of today. Rather, that it is the basis of a method which will support the introduction of progressive change both now and in the future.

Whereas the book tends to focus on describing the development and application of the method to a whole institution, the principles of the method are also appropriate for application to smaller, constituent parts of an institution, such as departments or even subdepartments, indeed a learning environment architecture is, in itself, a subset of a whole-institution architecture. In fact we would be quite surprised if many established HEIs made the decision to start to implement the methodology across the whole institution at one fell swoop. However, we believe that it will be important for an institution to take a corporate view of any projects that are started, albeit that they may at first be led by 'champions' at a lower level.

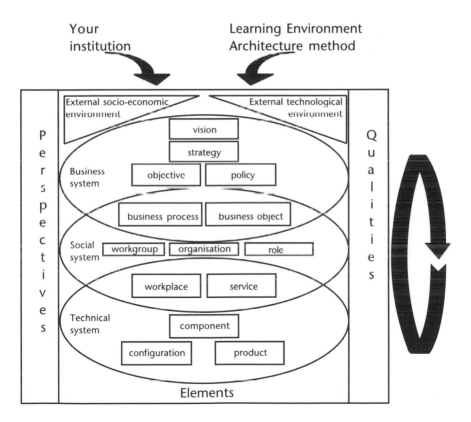

Figure 1.1 The Learning Environment Architecture method

Similarly this book's emphasis is clearly on the learning environment as it will be applied in the main to the undergraduate community, but this does not mean that we wish to understate the importance of postgraduate and research activities of HEIs. These will have a tremendous impact on a learning environment. We have taken this approach to keep the scope of the document to a manageable level; we hope our readers will be able to relate the principles of the method to these crucial areas.

Starting with business issues and trends, some of which are described in Chapter 2, you derive a set of implications which shape the institution's architecture. You choose which are the most important issues for your institution and add your own where appropriate.

Leading on from the issues and trends highlighted in Chapter 2, Chapter 3 examines the issue of managing change. This chapter first offers a method for setting the direction for an organisation which includes capturing the vision, and developing strategies, objectives and policies designed to realise it. Chapter 3 also explores how an HEI needs to consider the level at which it is going to approach change.

In developing an architecture for your institution it is important that, at each stage, you check how well it matches the needs of the people who are involved with it, both internally and externally. Chapter 4 looks at the learning environment from seven different perspectives, and how qualities are used to capture a value system for it.

Chapters 5 and 6 describe the key business objects and processes for a generic institution. Steered by your direction you should examine your business processes and, as necessary, develop them with the aid of the examples

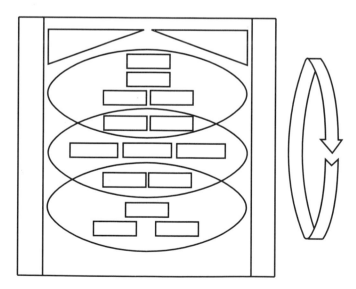

Figure 1.2 The chapter icon

given. These objects and processes form the links between the business and the social systems.

You should then model your institution's social system using the approach and examples provided in Chapter 7.

Chapter 8 illustrates how you map your social system to your supporting technical systems by considering the various workplaces you plan to support.

Chapter 9 helps you develop technical systems that support your institution's business needs by identifying a set of components which provide the required services.

The method diagram is used as an icon at the start of each chapter (Figure 1.2). You can see which part of the method is being covered in the chapter, by the shading on the icon.

What next?

This chapter has explained what the Learning Environment Architecture is about, its benefits and the overall method.

The method is a sequential process, although it is not necessary to complete each stage in great detail. However, we would always recommend that you do start with a direction-setting statement; then it will be better to define each part at a high level and iterate around the architecture loop, refining the stage you need developed in more detail. You may find that there is, for example, a particular key process that you wish to pursue in great detail before developing others.

Later, each stage needs to be revisited to check whether it is still valid, as changes may have occurred to the external environment or within the institution. The architecture must be updated as a part of an institution's key business process.

The next chapter looks at some of the issues facing learning institutions.

2

Business Issues and Trends

This chapter covers issues and trends in higher education. For each issue we identify the key pressures for change and the main implications for education. This format is intended to help you to address each of the issues and plan the necessary changes. Local issues will need to be incorporated to achieve a comprehensive institution architecture.

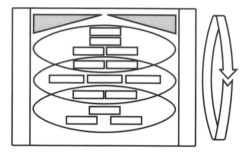

In recent years the higher education system in the United Kingdom has been experiencing an unprecedented rate of change. This has been evidenced most dramatically by a huge increase in student numbers, but more fundamental forces are at work which are transforming the very nature of higher education in this country. This is leading to intensive questioning of the purposes of higher education, and to a rethinking of the nature of the educational experience which is made available to students. In this chapter we attempt to describe the principal forces for change in higher education, and to specify how they are stimulating a demand for the creation of radically different learning environments.

At the present time, HEIs are facing many issues which require fundamental change at all levels, for example:

- Massification of education
- Competition and control
- Changing student profile
- Provision of learning resources.

Each issue puts pressure on learning institutions to incorporate new teaching and learning methods and to develop new learning environments which will better cope with these pressures.

The list is not all-inclusive. Each establishment will have a different priority and attitude to common trends and these will be linked to local issues and policy decisions. The reasons for including these issues are to demonstrate that a systematic approach can be adopted which defines the major components in an institution's architecture, and to act as a basis for examples of using the architecture method within the later sections of the book.

Massification of education

In a very short space of time higher education has changed from an elite system to one of mass participation, with over 30 per cent of 18-year-old school leavers entering higher education.

Pressures for change

The Committee of Vice-Chancellors and Principals has recently called for the participation rate in higher education to rise to 40 per cent by the year 2000. The massification of higher education has also been accompanied by the end of the divide between universities and polytechnics, doubling the number of universities. There is a great diversity of institutional missions which makes it difficult to produce one set of rules for the future direction of higher education institutions.

This rapid growth in higher education has happened against a background of falling revenue. Public sector funding per student has fallen by 27 per cent in the past five years and is likely to fall another 10 per cent, in real terms, over the next three years. This has placed enormous pressure on establishments to make efficiency gains, and while much has been achieved, there are signs of severe strain. Many institutions are also facing staffing problems caused by erosion of salary levels and employment benefits, and the proportion of staff on part-time or fixed-term contracts is increasing. All resources are being stretched and it is increasingly difficult to maintain conventional patterns of working and traditional models of teaching and learning.

Implications

Strategic decisions must be taken by learning institutions to determine what sort of learning environment they are going to provide, to how many students and where. These decisions will influence the services that are required and resources, including staff, will have to be used to create the most effective environment.

In order to gain the improvements in efficiency and effectiveness that massification demands, learning institutions will need to consider:

* New organisational structures
* New learning methods

- New delivery methods enhanced by information and communications technology
- New partnerships and collaborations.

Competition and control

Funding pressures and other factors mean that HEIs must now compete for both student and research income. In addition there are growing requirements for greater accountability in all areas of work.

Pressures for change

Although HEIs remain nominally independent and autonomous, the higher education system in Britain has become increasingly subject to central control, through the higher education funding councils set up by the government in 1993. Through control of the public purse, the funding councils have immense power to steer the system in different directions. In particular they are able to control the rate of expansion of the system, particularly at undergraduate level, with an extraordinary degree of precision, and they retain punitive powers to discipline any institution which attempts to ignore necessary constraints.

Largely in response to the perceived needs of industry there has been a shift away from discipline-focused degrees, in which subjects are studied for their own sake, towards acquisition of the kinds of skills which can be directly used in employment. Many degree programmes now offer modules in, for example, communication skills, learning skills, information-handling skills and information technology skills, or attempt to incorporate these directly into discipline-based teaching and learning. Students are increasingly asking the question 'How will this degree improve my opportunities of getting a job?'

Funding pressures and the increasing pressure from government and industry to encourage vocational learning, and other factors, mean that HEIs now inhabit an increasingly competitive environment.

The funding councils have also used their authority to introduce mechanisms of accountability and control over both teaching and research. HEIs are now subject to inspection to a degree unimaginable even five years ago.

Whatever the merits of quality assurance, funding councils have the potential to shift the system in new directions. This has been most explicit through the linking of funding to the outcome of the periodic research selectivity exercise. Although one of the short-term effects of this policy has been to promote interest in research activity across a wider than ever range of institutions, there is no disguising the tendency for research funds to be increasingly concentrated on an elite group of research-oriented HEIs.

It is more than likely that the assurance of teaching quality will soon be similarly linked to funding, and it is not impossible that the same institutions will benefit disproportionately, reinforcing the stratification as well as the diversity of the system.

The increasingly competitive environment in which HEIs find themselves means that they must now compete for both student and research income, whether this is derived from the funding councils, local authority tuition fees, private industry and other public sector agencies, or from students themselves.

Competition is likely to change the face of the new higher education sector considerably over the next decade. It is also likely to increase the diversity of the system, with implications for teaching and learning. We do not yet have a settled system, and we may never have one again.

Implications

In the face of this competition, learning institutions need to be asking certain questions to help define their future, for example:

- What are the investment factors that will determine how likely the institution is to acquire its funding?
- How will the balance be split between teaching and research?
- How important is teaching to a learning environment, how important is research?
- Is specialisation likely to lead to a satisfactory conclusion or will wider choice attract more students?
- Where are students likely to come from?
- What are students looking for?
- Are some students more financially attractive than others?
- Can we build a 'learning product' that will be attractive to them?
- Can we define and afford a learning infrastructure that will attract our target students?
- How do we publicise ourselves to our market?

At present, an HEI's fee structure is very coarse grained. Most charge a flat fee for each year enrolled, often irrespective of the student's actual usage of HEI resources. With increasing modularisation and the implementation of Credit Accumulation and Transfer Schemes (CATS), we can envisage a future where students will do most of their learning through an association with a number of different HEIs, accessing many of their resources from a distance over the Internet, or some other form of information superhighway. The demands such students will place on an HEI will vary substantially over time and students are likely to migrate away from those HEIs with cumbersome fee structure/access methods and towards those which allow the most flexible forms of access and payment, tied closely to resources used. In an increasingly competitive, though growing market for lifelong learning, HEIs will need to be prepared for the implementation, monitoring and collecting of fees which will not only need to be tightly coupled to the real costs of learning resources used by students but which will also need to be priced to offer perceived value to the students and prospective students.

As the market becomes more competitive, HEIs will increasingly have to adopt a typical service-based company marketing approach, one which takes account of the additional external statutory factors that industrial companies do not have to face.

Competition coupled with quality assurance means that learning institutions cannot just look for efficiency gains to cope with massification but must engage in continuous improvement of the effectiveness of their learning environments. The culture and value base of most, if not all, learning institutions will naturally encourage this.

Changing student profile

Much, if not most, attention is paid to the sheer increase in student numbers; but this disguises a more fundamental requirement for change that is reflected in a dramatic alteration in both the student profile and the student expectation.

Pressures for change

These changes can be traced, in part, to the incentive given by the government to expand the system. Student numbers could not be increased quickly enough by depending on the traditional A-level route, and the new channels set up have produced an influx of students entering via non-traditional routes. We now have more students over the age of 21 than under it, and more and more part-time students. In many institutions part-time students are now in the majority.

In educational terms, there has been a shift away from traditional models in which most students might have been viewed as passive recipients of teaching, absorbing information in an uncritical way. There is a growing enthusiasm for active, independent learning, which encourages deep, rather than surface, processing of information. This in turn requires a greater range of assessment methods.

In the competition for students, particularly postgraduate students who are not directly subject to the funding councils' control of numbers, learning institutions have been increasingly entering global educational markets, particularly in the currently lucrative Pacific Rim countries. Much of the provision is based on a combination of franchised teaching and distance learning. Again, this is changing the profile of the student population considerably, with significant implications for teaching and learning, and assessment.

HEIs have also become increasingly active nearer to home. In order to strengthen their regional positions, particularly in the light of a student funding regime which may force more students to study from home, learning institutions are entering into collaborative arrangements with a wide range of providers of secondary, higher and further education.

Franchising and other forms of collaboration are blurring the boundaries between HE and FE. The notion that higher education will be always provided on a physically identifiable campus to a homogeneous group of students is increasingly untenable as a vision of the future.

We must also continue to recognise the positive impact on learning that social interactivity unquestionably provides. Education can be conceived of as a process of transferring information, knowledge, or skills from teacher to learner. But it is also an intensely social process of induction into community. The larger community dominates in the early stages. The relevant communities become more and more specialised as the student matures. Undergraduate education always has been an induction into communities of 'graduates' and professionals with rights, powers, privileges, opportunities and responsibilities.

This trend is reinforced by a growing interest in lifelong learning and, particularly, in the integration of study and employment. Much of the impetus behind the expansion of HE has come from the demands of industry for a more relevant form of HE, whose graduates more closely match its recruitment needs – a factor which, increasingly, is influencing students' choice of learning institution. This factor is also reflected in the merger of the government Departments of Education and Employment. Current thinking about further expansion of the HE system is driven even more strongly by the idea of lifelong learning. As a part-time learner, or as a full-time student between employments, the graduate may continue to use the institution to further develop his skills, or improve his potential contribution to industry. One possible way of funding future expansion would be to reduce the initial period of HE to two years and to combine this with work-based lifelong learning. Such a move would have to be in partnership with industry and take account of entering more deeply into competition in the industrial training market.

Implications

Key institutional responses to these pressures are:

- Implementation of modularised degree structures
- Introduction of semesterisation
- Schemes for the uniform accreditation of learning
- Development of assessment methods that test skill and competences needed for employment and lifelong learning.

These have been adopted in the interests of incorporating greater range and flexibility into degree programmes, enhancing their attractiveness to students and making the programmes more adaptable to rapidly shifting external demands.

Modularisation has consequences of its own which can also have a radical impact, for example:

- Pressure on certain resources is accentuated at more frequent points in the academic year
- Traditional forms of assessment become more difficult to sustain within the unit of the single semester
- The structure lends itself to novel approaches to teaching and learning, thus in itself facilitating change
- In association with CATS, it opens up the possibility of students moving from one institution to another, being credited for prior learning and accumulating qualifications from multiple institution sources, probably over an unpredictable period of time.

Students are increasingly seeking learning environments which offer them more choice, not just of courses, but also of learning and assessment methods, of place of study as well as time and pace of study, suited to their individual learning styles and career aspirations. In offering students a choice, HEIs will need to consider offering learning environments which will include active, independent and distance learning systems. These can be dramatically enhanced, or indeed only made possible, by the application of modern information and communications technology – but at what and whose expense? For example, does the HEI have to provide all students with a suitable workstation capable of supporting multimedia courseware, with telephone access from their accommodation to SuperJANET and Internet – or can it be assumed that there will be a suitable student loan scheme which will be the provider? Currently the answer is probably 'No' to both questions. But if these new approaches constitute the only sustainable way of coping with a mass system of higher education, answers to funding questions will have to be found.

The changes which are accelerating in higher education are driven, in part, by the new necessities of teaching a wider range of students at different stages of their development with more diverse educational experience; they are also driven, in part, by these new technological possibilities of communication. Thinking about these changes has perhaps tended to focus on the first conception of education, as referred to under 'Pressures for change', as the transfer of information. Which innovations succeed and which fail will be chiefly determined in the second conception of education as a process of social induction. These factors are most affected by distance and open learning, and by the different life situations of students. The external social opportunities are also impacted by changes in patterns of employment.

The provision of learning resources

It is not possible to specify exactly what the learning environments of the future will look like, since they will reflect institutional diversity and will be the outcome of institutional choices. However, some general characteristics of the new environments can be identified.

Pressures for change

As we will continue to suggest throughout this book, HEIs are likely to move away from a pattern based on conventional teaching methods delivered in a fixed place at a fixed time, to a much more flexible system in which people learn how they want, when they want and where they want. Students will be independent, active learners, not passive recipients of teaching. They will make extensive use of technology in learning, and many of them will learn at a distance, from home or in the workplace, not on a campus at all. They will use an enormously wide range of learning resources: computer-based learning packages; printed open learning materials; networked information resources which they will seek out across the Internet; and books and other documents held in the library or resource centre. They will inhabit a much more diverse, richer information environment.

Implications

There are likely to be important shifts in the organisation of access to learning resources in the future. In particular, the role of the library as a principal storehouse of learning materials can be expected to diminish. In the past, everybody needed to come to the library, both to gain access to the materials stored there and to use the bibliographic tools – catalogues and other indexes – which gave information about what the library possessed. Most of the latter activity, i.e. access to metadata, can now be carried out from the desktop, and increasingly this is what is happening. The library does therefore experience some loss of control. It is no longer the institutional library which is at the centre of things, but the workstation on the desktop of the end-user. Furthermore, the electronic services offered by the library are only some among many of the information resources which the end-user can access. This has often been described as the modern equivalent of the Copernican revolution. The end-user, not the library, is now at the centre of the information universe, and the library is just one among many resources in orbit around that user.

This decentralisation of access to information is of course another aspect of the more general decentralisation of computing; the personalisation of computing which has destroyed the similarly Ptolemaic centrality of the mainframe.

There is another significant sense in which the library is becoming less important. Traditionally the library has provided an organising focus for the collection and provision of access to information resources. Some of these functions are now being carried out at a national level. This trend is likely to increase in importance. The ability of the higher education community in the UK to use top-sliced funds to act in the collective interest, and to invest in infrastructure and common services, is a major strength. The development of JANET and SuperJANET could not otherwise have occurred; now we are seeing a whole range of value-added services. A sizeable portfolio of datasets is being assembled by the JISC, hosted at a number of different data centres, and we are beginning to make a reality of what has been called the 'national distributed electronic collection'.

The movement towards national, community-wide provision applies not only to the collection of electronic material, but to organisation of access. Subject gateways, such as the Social Science Information Gateway, are being funded to support resource discovery and access, as well as to provide a measure of quality control.

So when it comes to the provision of access to electronic information resources, we are seeing a movement both outwards to the end-user and upwards to the national level. The central role of the library, both as a place and an organising focus, is being diminished.

The trend is repeated in the case of more general learning materials. The funding councils have invested close to £40 million in the Teaching and Learning Technology Programme (TLTP), which is designed to produce subject-based courseware packages which can be used right across the HE sector. Other initiatives, such as the Computers in Teaching Initiative (CTI) and the Open Learning Foundation (OLF), show the sector again acting collectively.

A further aspect that springs to mind when one considers the prospect of the wealth of access to, and subsequent distribution and use of, electronic information sources, is that of copyright. Institutions will need to consider how they will take steps to control this. Perhaps some sort of copyright advice and clearance unit will be required in every institution.

While the individual HEI remains the paramount focus for the organisation of higher education, the empowerment of the users of information systems, and the growing importance of collective action at a national level, are trends which cannot be ignored.

A view from within the sector

In this chapter we have presented our view of the key issues affecting the sector as a whole, which are creating great pressure for change in HEIs. Views and interpretations do vary, and we think it is valuable to look at some of the thinking recently expressed by the UK HEI community.

The report of the working party of the Committee of Scottish University Principals (1992), *Teaching and Learning in an Expanding Higher Education System*, often referred to as the MacFarlane Report, leads with the following statement:

> A fundamental appraisal of, and a radical approach to, the problems of teaching and learning in mass higher education is now necessary. While the scale of the changes required is such that an evolutionary form of

development is both inevitable and desirable, there is an urgent need to foster and introduce innovative approaches and structures, and to make the most effective use of new technology. These, however, can only supply part of the solution to the problems which higher education faces. The greatest challenge is to persuade a majority of those involved in higher education to see teaching as their prime activity, and as one posing intellectual challenges and offering rewards comparable to those of standard research. The development and imaginative use of shared educational resources, and the necessary research into learning processes and new forms of large-scale teaching, will all require new organisational structures and the creation of supporting infrastructures at national and institutional level.

(Committee of Scottish University Principals 1992: ix)

What next?

This chapter has analysed just a sample of the many issues facing HEIs. Each issue will be treated differently by different establishments, as each will have additional pressures to address. However, it is certain that traditional methods of teaching and learning in HE, based on the tutorial, the seminar, the lecture and the essay are becoming increasingly less relevant to the HE system which is now being created and which will be characteristic of the first decades of the twenty-first century.

In part, this is simply the result of the massification of the system. The conventional approaches to teaching are under extreme stress already, and many believe that standards are declining as a result. We simply do not have the resources to sustain the teaching environment characteristic of an elite system. There are not enough lecturers, library books or rooms, and there is not enough time. For these reasons we have no choice but to do things differently.

There is, however, a more profound reason for doing things differently, because we are not just facing increased numbers of students. In a hundred different ways, we are confronting a new student body, with new demands, new expectations and different learning styles. We are facing a transition to a much more flexible system in which people will demand to learn how they want, when they want and where they want. Many of them will learn at a distance, at home or in the workplace, not on the campus at all. Some of them will be learning on the other side of the world. It will not only be students who have different expectations, Government and industry will also be demanding a different type of graduate, one who is more capable of meeting the needs of industry and public service in the next century.

To a greater or lesser extent all HEIs face the challenge of developing new and more appropriate learning environments for the twenty-first century and we believe that the method described in this architecture will help you to achieve this.

The first task that you need to carry out to create a comprehensive architecture is to establish the key business pressures facing your HEI. These may include the examples above, and will certainly extend beyond them. Because the issues are documented a start can be made on working out the implications at both the business and the technical levels.

The next chapter looks at the management of change, how it is essential for you to establish a vision for your HEI so that everyone knows which direction the institution is heading in. A look at organisational transformation levels then follows, which will help you to find the right balance for implementation in your institution.

3

Managing Change

This chapter discusses how the architectural approach can be used in the process of managing change. It looks at the critical importance of establishing a vision for your institution as the key driver in determining your future direction, and at whether or not an evolutionary rather than revolutionary approach can be adopted.

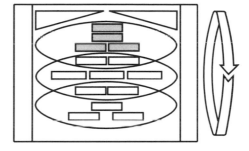

In the previous chapter we examined some of the major issues and trends driving change in the UK higher education sector today. In this chapter we examine how we should approach the management of change. The challenge is to create a situation where changes can be implemented to the maximum benefit of the institution with the lowest possible risk and cost – but it will not be without risk or cost. Change cannot be resisted or avoided and to attempt to do so will lead to inevitable decline. A planned approach that continuously assesses the needs for and implications of change, and implements policies to incorporate approved changes will place institutions in a much stronger position in the increasingly competitive world of higher education.

However, it should be stressed that implementing change for change's sake is not recommended and it may well be valid for a management team consciously to decide that it would be more appropriate, at a particular point in time, to keep their options for change 'strategically open'. The distinction between making such a decision and failing to make a decision at all must be recognised, and any such decision must take place within a planning process that incorporates continuous assessment and review.

The change management process

The process of managing change has four key stages which are brought together in the Learning Environment Architecture. The stages are shown in Figure 3.1. The large arrow indicates the iterative nature of the process.

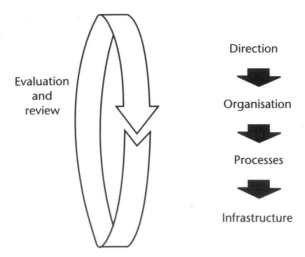

Figure 3.1 Managing change

This arrow has been labeled 'Evaluation and review' to indicate that within the process, all stages must incorporate some form of continuous assessment and appraisal.

Direction

An HEI must know where it is going. It needs to define its direction, which will include a vision statement, strategies, business objectives and policies.

An HEI must possess a vision of what it intends to be. That vision needs to embrace not only the services it intends to enable and provide, how and to whom it intends to provide them, but also the principles and values it wants to support and demonstrate. We discuss the process for capturing vision, and how it should be linked to strategy and objectives, later in this chapter.

The following extract from the December 1995 report *Guidelines for Developing an Information Strategy* from the JISC Information Strategy Steering Group (1995b: 10) is probably pertinent at this point:

> The task for the Vice-Chancellor/Principal is to set the agenda which will produce the set of attitudes which is the Information Strategy. He or she needs to ensure that the attitudes pervade the institution . . . The process . . . needs to embrace the whole community, it needs to be renewed in order to ensure that the institution's approach has kept up to date (in so far as this is necessary). And it needs to be monitored to ensure that the 'shared vision' is understood, genuinely shared and acted upon.

Organisation

In this context organisation includes not only the structure that the institution intends to put in place to deliver its vision, but also its relationships to the organisations, groups and individuals who influence it or are influenced by it. We look at the subject of organisation as part of the institution's social system in Chapter 7.

Processes

An HEI must understand which core processes it needs to put in place. These processes must be designed to support the objectives of the business. Achieving the objectives must not be subservient to the processes. In other words, processes that do not contribute to the achievement of the stated objectives of an institution will require examination to determine whether they can be modified or need to be replaced.

This will have to be balanced with an understanding of the people-centred nature of an HEI. For example, it could be argued that research is as much about the development of the knowledge of the researcher as it is about short-term research results. This could be a reflection of the principles and values incorporated in setting the direction.

We look in some detail at the processes in a learning environment in Chapter 6.

Infrastructure

The infrastructure supports the day-to-day operation of the HEI. Infrastructure includes all the institution's resources such as buildings, technology such as voice and data networks, laboratory equipment, IT systems, and all the people that use them. The infrastructure is aligned to the business system and supports the business processes of the institution.

Planning principles

The following principles need to be applied:

- The four stages must be viewed as aspects of a coherent whole
- It is likely that the approach will be evolutionary, not revolutionary. Major change, especially where it involves changing the existing culture of the organisation, can usually only be achieved in several planned and monitored steps. Conversely, some gains may only be possible by taking a revolutionary approach

- Build in flexibility to cope with further change in the future. Strategies need to cope with the legacy of the past, in terms of both culture and systems
- Each stage needs to be decided, documented and communicated to all parties involved before implementation
- The process is an iterative one. We suggest that you do not attempt to pursue each stage for too long. Focus on the priorities and work through the process at this level so others can be picked up at the next iteration. Also, as we have established, any plan should be kept up to date to accommodate change.

Setting direction

We have discussed at some length the driving forces for change and some of the possible changes that HEIs need to consider today. Before an HEI can decide which changes to make, which strategies to put in place and which architectures to create, it needs to have set its direction of change.

The direction of change and eventual goal of the institution are encapsulated in its vision. A vision needs to reflect the basic beliefs and core values of the institution. It is tempting to say 'and its culture' at this point, but in a world of change, organisational cultures often have to be at least challenged if not actually forcefully changed, and we may have to revisit our beliefs and core values to make sure that we are really sure we understand what they are.

What is a vision?

Definitions of vision in an organisational context vary, of course, and there are many examples. Here is one that we feel is worth repeating:

> A vision defines an enterprise's purpose. It should present an attractive and clear view of the future that can be shared.
>
> (Sir John Harvey-Jones)

It is important to develop a simple statement of your vision that represents the true values and ambitions of your institution.

A number of attributes are common to a successful vision:

- Beliefs and values
- Direction
- Timescale
- Motivation.

Beliefs and values
If a vision is to be effective in guiding the institution, it must accurately reflect the institution's core values and beliefs. The vision must be concerned with

the institution's ethical values. There need not be just a single statement of beliefs and core values, there might be a number of them.

For example an institution might make the following statements of beliefs and core values, on which to base its vision:

- 'It is our goal to foster the development of a learning society'
- 'We want to be renowned for the quality of our learning environment, measured by the quality of our graduates'
- 'We aim to be regarded as one of the best-balanced research and learning institutions.'

Care will be needed to ensure that these accurately reflect the institution's beliefs and values, and also that they are not merely a collection of vacuous statements.

Direction
The vision should provide direction for the institution. Because a vision defines an aiming point it should, usually, be stated simply and concisely. A vision does not need to state how the aiming point should, will or can be reached, nor need it include a statement of the current state, but it must be soundly based on the belief that there is a practical path that can be found to reach it.

By setting the direction the vision sets the context in which decisions are made, indicating what choices should be made at each decision point. All decisions should be made with the vision in mind.

Figure 3.2 illustrates simply how a vision gives direction for the institution and how it helps with decision making in evolving the strategies that follow.

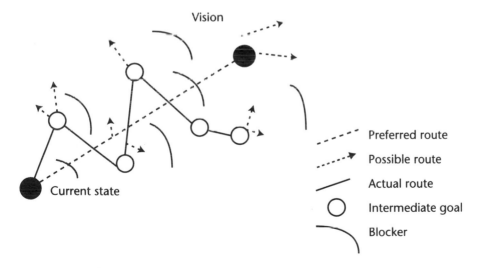

Figure 3.2 Importance of vision in direction setting

It also suggests that, in the real world, there will be very real blockers to the preferred route which will have to be circumvented even if the choice appears to move tangentially away from the envisioned direction. It also suggests that there are likely to be intermediary goals which will be more practically attainable and, as this must be an iterative process, over time you will need to revisit the vision and, if necessary, modify it.

Timescale

Fundamental changes of attitudes, direction, strategy and culture do take time to achieve. The vision therefore needs to be set at some appropriate distance in the future: not so close that it becomes simply a local goal, but not so far that it seems to be a futuristic fantasy.

Timescales can be set very precisely (for example to a particular year) or more openly (for example by the end of the decade), or they can be tied to match a particular event, such as 'when SuperJANET is installed in all UK HEIs'.

Motivation

One essential in setting vision is to ensure that the entire organisation is motivated very strongly towards its achievement. This means it must be communicable and communicated to all. This may well influence the clarity and achievability (or challenge) of the vision statement.

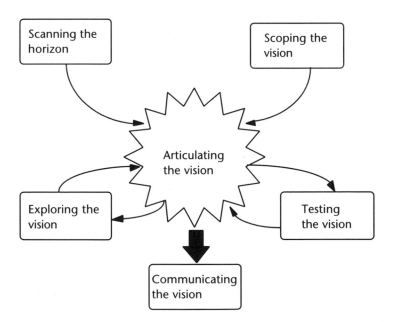

Figure 3.3 Articulating the vision

Capturing vision

Figure 3.3 represents a model of how a vision can be captured. We briefly explain the stages below. Any reader who would like to explore them in more detail will find Brown (1994) useful.

- *Scanning the horizon* – find out as much as possible about the environment in which the institution operates, about visions held by other institutions and competitors and by other organisations with which the institution has dealings
- *Scoping the vision* – determine what the area for competitive behaviour is going to be, to set the scope and focus of the vision and the resulting strategies
- *Articulating the vision* – develop a concise, clear simple statement of the vision, with supporting details describing the vision and the business needs it is intended to satisfy
- *Exploring the vision* – investigate in depth the consequences of the vision: what will the future be like if the vision is adopted? This is a repetitive process, as initial thoughts will need to be revised if the assessment of the future picture proves to be unacceptable
- *Testing the vision* – assess how much of a challenge the vision will present to the institution, whether it can be translated into real strategies and whether it matches the goals and aspirations of the people who will be affected by it. This is also a repetitive process that requires revision depending on how you expect it will translate into achievable strategies, matched by personal goals. It will be necessary to revisit the vision from time to time to validate that it continues to reflect accurately the institution's purpose
- *Communicating the vision* – decide how best to communicate the vision throughout the institution, to students, other customers and trading partners.

Evolving business strategy

A business strategy should refine the vision of the institution, expressing it as a statement of objectives and critical success factors. The objectives should cover all aspects of the institution and its business.

The main goal of the business strategy is to direct how the different players associated with the institution must operate if the vision is to be achieved. The business strategy should incorporate the technical strategy so that decisions about technology directly relate to the business objectives and the institution's vision.

Who produces the business strategy?

It will be necessary to set up a strategy planning team for the institution. The team will usually have representatives from all parts of the institution, and members must be able to understand the need to view the institution's requirements from the following perspectives:

- Enterprise manager (vice-chancellor, dean, head of department, council members)
- Staff (teaching, research and support)
- Student (under- and postgraduate)
- Funding agencies (HEFC, research council)
- Other trading partners (industry, professional associations, publishers).

Team members must be comfortable in dealing with business and technical issues at an appropriate level. It must be recognised that the team members' attitude to innovation and evolution will have a significant impact on the strategy finally produced.

Figure 3.4 represents the method for evolving a business strategy, followed by a brief summary of the key factors. If you wish to find out more about this method, we recommend Gale (1994).

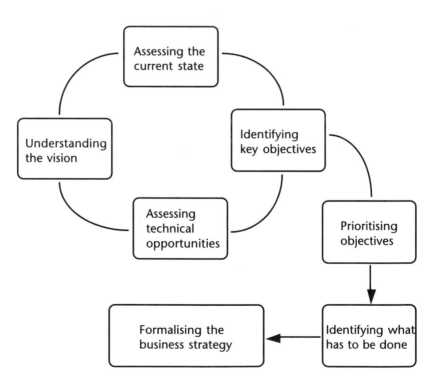

Figure 3.4 Evolving a business strategy

Understanding the vision

The role of an institution's vision is to provide direction and motivation for the people associated with the institution. The strategy planning team has to turn the statements in the vision into concrete proposals for action. To do this the team must share a common understanding of the vision and, in particular, of the following issues:

- *Scope of the business change* – the scope of the change envisaged in the vision statement includes the parts of the institution which will be affected, the costs, risks and timescales which would be constraints in implementing the changes
- *Attitude to change* – the attitude of the strategy team towards the proposed changes is also important. For example, the team has to agree whether radical innovation is required and whether the vision can be achieved by evolving from the current state
- *Trading relationship model* – the team should be encouraged to construct trading relationship models which summarise the team's view of how the institution will operate if the changes are implemented.

    For trading partners, collect as much intelligence as you can about the following aspects:
    - What added value does each trading partner offer? Are they the added values that the enterprise needs?
    - What channels are there? Is there potential for opening up new channels using the current or other trading partners?
    - What use is being made of trading partners in the area of research. Is there scope for sharing more?
    - What are the institution's service relationships with trading partners? Are they effective? Would any other services be beneficial?

Assessing the current state

Strategic change should be based on the current strengths of the institution and should attempt to deal with perceived weaknesses.

The process must take account of the legacy of the past investment into the existing assets of the institution (people skills, lecture theatres, libraries, laboratories, systems, etc.). No institution is going to implement change by instantly discarding all that has gone on before. Apart from anything else, this would be simply unaffordable. There will inevitably be some changes that will require revolutionary steps to be taken if the resulting benefits are to be achieved at all. More practically, though, even where it will incorporate some revolutionary concepts, change will be progressively applied through carefully laid and continuously monitored transition plans making the best use of existing assets during transition. This area of activity should generate the following outputs:

- *Asset model* – the team should construct an asset model to describe the assets the institution has. The model should identify the core assets (those which are vital to the business) and also those which could be traded as part of the strategic change. The decision on whether an asset is core or non-core depends on the vision of the institution. The asset model represents the strategy planning team's view of which of the institution's many assets are core to the business, and which are non-core. Later on decisions have to be made about how non-core assets are used and how core assets will be protected and developed
- *Strengths and weaknesses* – the team should assess the strengths and weaknesses based on their own understanding of the current operation and on their perception of how these are viewed internally and externally
- *Scenarios* – the team should begin to develop scenarios to describe their view of how the institution will look if the proposed changes are implemented. A scenario is simply a formalised documentation of the envisaged situation.

Assessing technical opportunities

Changes in technology, and the use of technology, can present opportunities for an institution – for example, new ways of doing the job not otherwise possible, new service opportunities, new levels of cost or new relationships with partners. A greater understanding of such opportunities could also expose threats to the institution – for example, foreign institutions with distance learning offerings.

This activity should help the team to evaluate the range of technical change that is envisaged within the timescales of the business strategy and to recommend which changes the strategy should accommodate. These technical changes should then be applied to the scenarios, for example if the institution were to consider providing distance-taught students with a personal, workstation-based, video conferencing facility. This could potentially provide a high quality tutoring service to these students, but such a decision would have a very significant impact on many other elements of the institution's business, social and technical systems including:

- *Budgets and cost* – this would not be a cheap option
- *Tutor time management* – would this be supported by the traditional appointment system and/or on-call time slots?
- *Communications network strategy* – what bandwidth will be required to support acceptable image and voice quality? How much concurrent access is to be offered?

Identifying key objectives

Each change that is envisaged by the strategy planning team represents a potential objective for the business strategy. The team should determine which are the key objectives implied by the scenarios and decide which should be included or excluded.

Objectives may be selected for a number of reasons – for example, to develop core assets, to build on strengths, to remove weaknesses, to exploit technical opportunities. The decisions are usually based on cost, benefit, risk assessment, and timescales.

Prioritising objectives

The key objectives chosen by the team will be based on a very wide consideration of potential change as directed by the vision and understood by the team. Objectives which appear to make a major contribution to several of the perspectives should be given high priority. The team should update the scenarios to show the benefits of adopting the high priority objectives.

Identifying what has to be done

To clarify what has to be done the team has to define the critical success factors for the achievement of high priority objectives and agree measures for achieving them.

Formalising the business strategy

The business strategy is defined in terms of:

- Mission (derived from vision statement)
- Objectives
- Critical success factors.

The scenarios can be used to develop ways to present the strategy to staff, students, funding councils, trading partners and any others.

Information technology and change

One of the most comprehensive investigations ever undertaken into organisational change and the role of information technology was *Management in the 1990s Research Program* (MIT90s), a major five-year international research programme. The programme was carried out by the Massachusetts Institute of Technology Sloan School of Management, published in 1990 and sponsored by major US and UK companies and US government departments. For further information see Morton (1991).

The MIT90s research suggests that business turbulence and technological change imply potential organisational change and that the external forces associated with environmental turbulence must be reacted to for survival. It proposes that information technology (IT) offers organisations the opportunity to react constructively. It further suggests that IT is not just a simple set of tools that an organisation can use for support but one that can alter the way work is done and that can shrink the effects of both time and space. Consider the following 1984 quotation from Diebold in the report:

> Information Technology is becoming increasingly the key to national economic well being, affecting virtually every industry and service. One would be hard pressed to name a business that does not depend on the effective use of information: to design products and services, to track and respond to market demands, or to make well informed decisions. Information technology will change the world more permanently and more profoundly than any technology so far seen in history and will bring about a transformation of civilisation to match.
>
> (MIT/Sloan 1990: 105)

Such a fundamentally powerful tool as IT is best deployed by those with enough vision to see what it can realistically mean to the organisation. In short, general management, preferably senior general management, should be in direct control of the pace and direction of its use. Strategy has traditionally been thought to exist at three levels: corporate, business unit and function. Historically, IT has been considered one of the support functions and as an administrative expense rather than a business investment. Thus senior general management must first align the three levels of strategy and then reposition IT from its historical support function to where it can play a critical role in strategy formulation and implementation.

The MIT90s research suggests that IT-enabled business reconfiguration is an evolutionary process and can be thought of as consisting of five stages, as shown in Figure 3.5.

Business transformation levels

In Figure 3.5 levels 1 and 2 are primarily concerned with improving current practice and can, therefore, be realised by adapting existing processes. Levels 3, 4 and 5, on the other hand, require a redefinition of function and purpose. They cannot easily, if at all, be achieved without establishing new processes.

Here are some examples of these five levels of transformation applied to learning environments.

Localised exploitation

The MIT90s report (p. 108) defines stage 1 as 'characterised by localised exploitation. In this stage IT is exploited within existing, isolated business

Degree of business
transformation

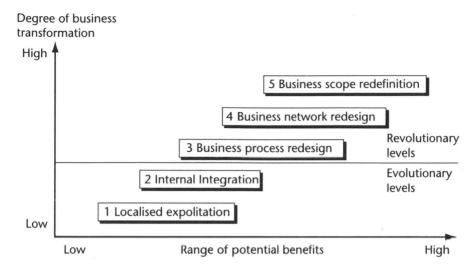

Figure 3.5 Business transformation levels (based on MIT/Sloan 1990: 107)

activities, normally within one function.' As is to be expected, this is the most widespread form of adaptation since it requires only a slight adaptation to current processes. Examples include the modification of courses to include small elements of learning technology, or the introduction of computer-based learning packages for student use in libraries. In the former example the process of course design, assessment and examination requires but slight change. In the latter the new material is treated as simply an extension of the resources on offer.

Internal integration

MIT90s (p. 111) suggests that stage 2 'can be thought of as building the internal electronic infrastructure that permits the integration of tasks, processes and functions. Stage 2 is a necessary condition if the investments in stage 1 are ever to be exploited.' This level of transformation is reached where the use of learning technology resources in libraries is designed into courses in the same way as the use of paper-based library resources. To enable this it may be necessary to create a unified information services structure incorporating library, computer centre and media services. It is certainly assisted by the drawing up of institution-wide strategies for information and for teaching and learning.

The combination of stages 1 and 2 is the springboard for the three remaining stages: stages 3, 4 and 5 are not necessarily sequential.

Business process redesign

Again, MIT90s (p. 115) suggests that stage 3 'results from a fundamental rethinking of the most effective way to conduct business'. When associated with a new approach to course design, the move towards the modularisation of courses and the associated arrangements for credit accumulation and transfer is an example of business process redesign. It demands a new approach to course design and information management which cannot successfully be achieved without establishing new business processes. The benefits of the transformation are, however, significant as flexibility of provision is greatly enhanced, enabling the needs of a wider range of students to be more closely met.

Business network redesign

MIT90s (p. 119) defines stage 4 as 'the use of IT by the organisation to include suppliers, customers or any other trading partner to contribute to the organisation's effectiveness. In a sense one is moving from the traditional, formal organisation, to a "virtual" or "networked" organisation that works together to accomplish a particular purpose.' The modularisation of courses creates a structure in which the distinction between full-time and part-time study can lose much of its significance. If modularisation is accompanied by a wholesale shift towards resource-based learning in place of lecture-based learning, then the distinction between local and distance learning becomes somewhat spurious as well. An institution that ended the distinction between full-time and part-time courses of study and between campus-based and distance education would have completed a process of business network redesign.

Business scope redefinition

MIT90s (p. 123) defines stage 5 as 'where an organisation decides to break out and exploit the new technology in the marketplace. The aim is to explain the logic underlying the composition of the organisation's portfolio of businesses, identify differential strategic thrusts and develop criteria for allocation of scarce resources among the businesses. Considerations of business scope dictate major strategic activities such as diversification, divestment, consolidation and mergers and acquisitions.' This, the highest level of business transformation, calls for a full reassessment of the role of HEIs. Such a reassessment might take as its starting point that the fundamental aim of an HEI is to meet the educational needs of individuals, groups and societies. There is no predetermined way of serving this aim, though there are various constraints, including the need for HEIs to function effectively as businesses. Radical rethinking of aims and the ways that they may be served can lead to a redefinition of the scope of the HEI's activity.

One possible outcome of the redefinition of the business scope of an HEI would be to identify core activities:

- *Creation of learning resources* – refer to page 78 for an elaboration of how this process could be managed
- *Delivery of learning resources* – while some lecturing might be retained it would no longer be the dominant form of learning support. Subsequent chapters discuss the diversity of approaches possible and the variety of locations where study can take place
- *Management of learning* – a resource-based approach to the provision of education gives rise to the need for an efficient system for managing both the learning resources and student learning. Students will require additional guidance to navigate the system
- *Assessment of learning* – this key function of HEIs is likely to change least. Methods of assessment will be modified to reflect the changing modes of student learning but institutions will continue to act as arbiters of academic standards. It is likely, however, that in future they will need to do this in conjunction with other HEIs (and other agencies, e.g. employers, NCVQ) to ensure comparability.

The process of scope redefinition would be further developed by:

- *Assessing the physical, human and intellectual resources available to the HEI* – institutions need to increase the return on their investments. Existing resources can be managed more effectively (for example annual repetition of lecture courses by academic staff is wasteful of their time and capabilities), and resources owned by students (study space, computers, facilities at work) can be exploited to augment the institution's own facilities
- *Assessing the market at local, regional, national and international levels* – with developments in communication technologies, higher education is becoming globalised and new markets, both local and distant, are emerging. HEIs must understand the markets open to them if they are to develop products which will appeal to new types of student
- *Identifying strategies for exploitation that maximise quality and minimise costs* – competition at all levels is likely to intensify so strategies that offer competitive advantage will be needed. Institutions are likely to be most successful if they build on existing strengths. This is likely to lead to increased diversification across higher education and specialisation within institutions.

In the transition period between provision of conventionally taught courses and the existence of a diverse learning environment, both approaches to student learning need to be supported simultaneously. This is a serious impediment to business scope redefinition and implies a need for significant investment to enable the transition to be made. The future learning environment integrates support services into the other activities, so ensuring a close match between needs and provision.

The National Council for Education Technology (NCET) has done some work based on the MIT90s research and has recently published a booklet called *Managing IT – a Planning Tool for Senior Managers* (NCET 1995), along with two brochures, one directed at schools and the other at further and higher education institutions. Each contains a matrix which enables an institution manager to position the institution's current implementation of IT against the five stages of business transformation. The NCET terms these stages: localised, coordinated, transformative, embedded and innovative, and classifies them into three groups, namely, evolutionary (stages 1 and 2), transitional (stage 3) and revolutionary (stages 4 and 5).

What next?

This chapter has looked at the question of how to manage change and, although it gives no absolute recommendations, by implication it will be necessary for HEIs to consider implementing some changes which will require taking on transformation at stage 3 and above. This will involve examining the value of current processes and certainly lead to a requirement to define and implement new ones. The next chapter looks at how you should view the learning environment from the different perspectives of the people involved and at the need to base it on an appropriate value system.

Chapters 5 and 6 explore the concept of business objects and suggest a process model for a learning environment.

4

Perspectives and Qualities

This chapter draws on the perspectives of seven different groups of people as a means of establishing a value system for the learning environment. This value system is expressed as five qualities to define quantifiable goals for the learning environment. This helps to ensure that the needs of these different groups are taken into account.

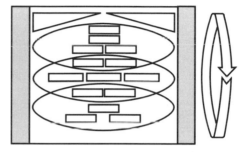

An institution architecture is a model of an HEI that enables change to be managed. It includes business, social and technical systems architectures to ensure that the changes to these systems are aligned at all times. Since each institution is different, each requires its own unique architecture. This chapter shows you how to produce the overall structure for your architecture.

The scope of the architecture considered in this book is restricted to the institution's learning environment. While this is clearly a key part of every HEI it does not cover other aspects of an institution, for example the living and social environments.

An institution's architecture is influenced significantly by the external environment which is, itself, under constant change. This was discussed in Chapter 2. While many of the external pressures are felt by all HEIs, internal pressures are all different because HEIs have their own cultures, their own specialities and so on.

Institutions already have many of the parts of an institution architecture. However, these are often loosely defined, generally scattered thinly about the organisation and rarely brought together. In this form, they are not a firm base from which to manage change. By developing an architecture as described in this book you create an asset for the organisation by causing convergence and creating synergy.

The Learning Environment Architecture supplies a generic architecture which you can adapt for your institution. The approach, which was introduced in Chapter 1, describes an architecture using three key concepts: perspectives, qualities and elements.

Perspectives and qualities are described in the following sections, where we provide templates to enable you to create your own institution architecture. Elements are described in Chapters 5 to 9.

Perspectives

The perspectives capture the key aspects of the learning environment viewed by different sets of people both within and outside the organisation. One set of people are concerned with the institution as a whole, and the other set are primarily concerned with the technical systems supporting the institution. This is represented in Figure 4.1.

There are many technical systems employed in a learning environment. The buildings used to house both students and staff are one such system. The electrical, plumbing, air conditioning and heating systems are further examples. The Post Office, TV and radio broadcasting and the telephone are still further examples. While the approach presented in this book is applicable to all these technical systems, we concentrate specifically on those technical systems which support the capture, manipulation and communication of information.

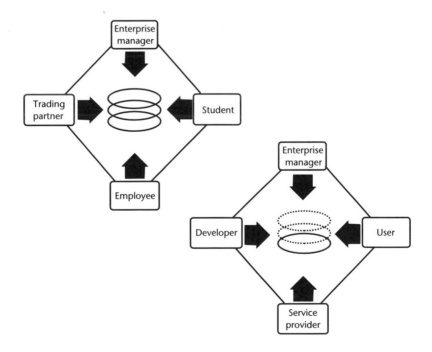

Figure 4.1 Perspectives of the learning environment

Enterprise manager

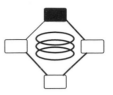

The enterprise manager perspective is common to both the business system and the technical system. The enterprise managers of an institution include, for example, the vice-chancellor and the deans. Other managers will also be included depending on the structure of the institution, especially those responsible for management of resources and services, such as finance, estates and information services.

Within an institution, enterprise management is under pressure to:

- Respond quickly and frequently to changing requirements
- Maintain the quality of learning while increasing its student numbers and managing its costs
- Be accessible to funding councils and other stakeholders
- Manage the expectations of the different stakeholders
- Balance competing internal demands for scarce resources, for example between faculties, between faculties and central services, and between activities such as teaching and research
- Solve diverse pressing short-term problems, while maintaining a consistent strategic direction.

As far as the learning environment is concerned, the response to these pressures is framed around:

- More flexible forms of teaching and learning
- Active learning, which holds the promise of improving the quality of learning by changing the student from a passive receiver of teacher-transmitted material to an active participant exercising choice over what, where, when and how they learn. This unlocks the student as a resource to support not only their own learning but also that of their peers
- Resource-based learning
- Off-campus provision
- Staff development
- Cooperative teaching provision (for example franchising).

Student

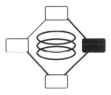

There is an increasingly diverse student body. Less than 50 per cent now fit the stereotype incoming student of a school leaver with A levels. The examples of key student needs seem to fall into four groups, as presented below – you can add or delete items to make it relevant to your institution.

Flexibility and choice
- Choice over the what, where, when, how of learning, and over the pace at which learning takes place
- Freedom to shape their own learning objectives and influence methods of learning and assessment, in an understanding, supportive environment
- Flexibility in all aspects of learning provision, enabling easy access for different student groups
- Opportunities to apply understanding. These may involve practice, work placement and so on, and the involvement of a wider range of supporters, including coaches and work placement mentors
- Flexibility of award (title, duration, level, possibility of dual academic/ vocational qualification).

Meaningful assessment
- Credit for prior experience and learning
- Assessment on entry to define skills, etc. on which further work is needed and identification of preferred learning style
- Timely, constructive feedback at an appropriate level of detail from a variety of sources including learning materials, technology, self, peers, academic staff, other staff and others outside the immediate learning environment
- Opportunities to review work (check understanding) with appropriate tutors to quantify performance and to identify and overcome problem areas
- Assessment both formative and summative, formal and informal.

Access to resources and information
- Detailed information on available learning resources with the opportunity to visit the institution and its learning managers to discuss these further and, once enrolled, continuous guidance in identifying and selecting from available opportunities
- Access to learning for both traditional A level students and more mature students with prior work histories and possibly no A level qualifications
- Access to adequate learning resources and advice on how best to use them
- Lecturers and an institution which appreciate the changes in the external environment, ensuring access to the most appropriate learning resources
- Knowledge of links the institution has with industry, and opportunities to gain practical work experience.

Support
- Easy, flexible access to various types of support to help achieve the agreed learning outcomes. These include tutorial, mentoring, counselling and guidance support services
- Help in acquiring learning skills, personal transferable skills and employability skills
- Access to personal support, not necessarily from someone related to the learning unit, to discuss learning objectives, problems, actions needed, and so on

- Advice and guidance on finance and housing
- Support for finding employment or further higher education opportunities once the current stage of learning is completed
- Links with industry (for example projects, sponsorship and work experience)
- Credible, informative and fair accreditation, recognition of achievements, stimulation, and timely resolution of queries
- A comfortable and enjoyable environment in which to learn including social facilities.

Employee

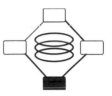

The academic staff of an institution have complex working lives which require them to balance the conflicting demands of several distinct roles (described in Chapter 7). This applies to all staff: academic, library, computing and administrative. The role of the academic is, probably, most complex and least well defined.

Academic staff have seen considerable change in the nature of their jobs in the last decade. The future seems certain to bring further change. Academics will, for example, be seen as developers of learning resources and managers of learning rather than the conduit through which knowledge flows to the student. Staff working in learning support (e.g. library and computing) are likely to play an increasingly significant role in the direct support of student learning.

These changes mean that academic staff are likely increasingly to become:

- *Team workers* because while they are reluctant to relinquish the right to design all aspects of the courses they teach, this is too labour intensive. Increased reuse of previously developed building blocks in the assembly of learning resources will improve efficiency. The national learning materials initiatives such as the Teaching and Learning Technology Programme and the Open Learning Foundation have developed such blocks, but further collaborative effort between institutions to promote wider reuse is needed
- *Business managers* because of the need to compete in an open market for students and funding
- *Technology-aware* because IT is being used increasingly in the learning environment as a means to achieve efficiency and quality gains. The Teaching and Learning Technology Support Network (TLTSN), the Computers in Teaching Initiative and other similar programmes are providing some of the necessary support infrastructure to facilitate this change
- *Multi-skilled* because the need to change and be flexible will require managers to have a range of skills that can be applied to the changing tasks in which they become involved. Alternatively they are likely to become . . .
- *Specialists* because of the different expertise needed in roles demanded of academic staff. It is difficult for all individuals to become multi-skilled, so

some HEIs have set up teams of specialised workgroups, for example administrators, counsellors, learning resource developers, etc.

- *Lifelong learners* themselves, being able to react to continuous change and to prepare for major institutional change. The Open Learning Foundation, Universities and Colleges Staff Development Agency (UCoSDA) and the Staff Education and Development Association work to raise the profile of staff development in HEIs.

Similar points apply to other staff. The general trend is towards:

- Team working across traditional barriers
- The capacity to use technology to support both their own work and student learning
- The development of new specialisms.

Trading partner

The trading partner perspective is the one that reflects the rich and varied set of external relationships that have to be managed by an institution. Chapter 2 suggests how these relationships are going to increase with time.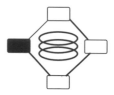

The themes that underlie partnerships with an institution are:

- *Enabling* – the institution puts in place the infrastructure that allows other organisations to contribute to the development of its learning environment
- *Commissioning* – the institution commissions work to be done in the development of its learning environment
- *Regulatory* – the institution is responsible for monitoring the quality of its learning environment and meeting financial constraints imposed primarily by the funding councils.

The following are examples of the types of relationships that have to be managed by an institution:

- *Funding bodies* – these provide funding for student places and maintain quality control mechanisms to ensure that the learning experience is of an adequate standard. They act as agents for the Government in setting economic, social and learning quality goals for an institution. As the quality of learning becomes more effectively measured the economic consequences of an inadequate learning environment will become increasingly detrimental to an institution
- *Committee of Vice-Chancellors and Principals* – the CVCP, while it has no direct trading relationship with the institutions, does have influence over them and also with funding bodies and the government. The CVCP leads the dialogue over the future shape of HEIs; this dialogue is a major driving force in the development of learning environments
- *Research councils* – research councils are becoming increasingly relevant in a regulatory role at postgraduate level. This influence will become more

pervasive as boundaries between undergraduate, taught postgraduate and postgraduate research work continue to soften

- *Industry and professional associations* – such organisations heavily influence the quality of learning in a number of subject areas through the accreditation process. Employers will increasingly influence students' preparatory learning both directly and indirectly. They will influence learning directly by work placement and commissioning the development of learning, and indirectly, by influencing the government, funding bodies and others
- *Other HEIs* – relationships with other HEIs have always existed and these will continue in a number of areas, such as development of joint courses, shared resources, student exchange and so on
- *Publishers* – publishers are increasingly concerned about HEIs' moves towards the use of electronic publications, and about how to deliver services which will preserve their copyright, royalty payments, and so on
- *Systems integrators* – the new learning environments will increasingly include networked workstations delivering video on demand, interactive CAL, interpersonal communication, computer-mediated group working and conferencing, and electronic information to the desktop. The development and ongoing maintenance, ensuring harmonisation, of all the components in a cost-effective manner is complex and systems integrators will have a vital role to play
- *Multimedia professional services* – multimedia consultants and production houses will facilitate the development of multimedia courseware providing institution-wide coordination, and setting standards for tools and presentation. They are a catalyst to promote a culture change where academics become as comfortable developing and using multimedia courseware as they are currently in writing textbooks and using blackboards and overhead projectors
- *Information and communication technology suppliers* – ICT suppliers see HEIs not only as potential customers for their products, but also as a source of recruitment of graduates like any other industry, and as the source for future influencers and decision makers in the use of technology across all sectors of business, both public and private. Most have an interest in encouraging the successful use and development of leading edge technologies as enablers in the learning environment, and will want to work in partnership with HEIs who seek to do this, often to the immediate benefit of the HEI.

User

The users of the technical system supporting the learning environment include the students and many of the roles performed by institution staff. The user perspective has, therefore, already been covered under student and 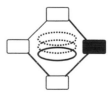 employee perspectives, above. Analysis of key business processes (as described in Chapter 6) establishes more detailed user requirements.

Service provider

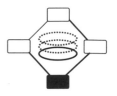

When looking at the service provider perspective, you should do so from the perspective of all services required by the learning environment, for example, laboratory technical support and audio/visual support as well as IT. The following questions are suggested from the perspective of an information systems service provider, as an example, but many of these will be common to all service provision:

- Is there a clearly defined process for measuring the quality of the service provided, for example are service level agreements implemented?
- Is there an agreed change control process?
- Is information systems provision regarded as an integral and important element of institution strategies and policies?
- Is adequate provision made to allow the information systems to be scalable, kept up to date and, in general, able to cater for change?
- Is there a process which will encourage and support the evaluation of technical innovation aligned to the business and pedagogic needs of the learning environment?

Developer

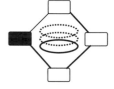

Development of the learning environment is a complex task involving many people from the HEI itself and from outside. The task is achieved by splitting it into parts and allocating responsibility for these parts to different people, who may well come from different departments. The different parts remain interdependent (as discussed in more detail in Chapter 6) and require careful coordination.

Even within a department the development task is likely to include many different types of developer responsible for the different development needs: changing processes, changing roles, changing technology, changing business objectives and so on. Additionally, people involved in the development are not all based at the same site and do not work for the same organisation, so the institution will need to establish effective ways of managing distributed group working.

Developers in general need group working support for team-based development, particularly where the members of the team are not based at the same site and where not all members are institution staff; they also need planning support, to help them prioritise and schedule the many interrelated development activities.

Learning material developers need knowledge resource access and authoring tools, etc.

Learning infrastructure developers need systems integration knowledge, tools and experience; telecommunications knowledge and experience; networking knowledge and experience, etc.

Qualities

A value system defining and quantifying the goals of a learning environment is expressed using the five OPEN*framework* qualities. These qualities are shown in Figure 4.2.

If you are planning change in an institution's learning environment, you need to be able to set realistic goals, measure progress against them, and confirm that they have been achieved. We suggest a structure for doing this, based on five qualities: availability, usability, performance, security, and potential for change. The qualities are a set of yardsticks used to measure different aspects of the business, social and information systems, in terms everyone involved can clearly understand. You can also use them to set specific goals for where you want your learning environment to get to, at a particular time in the future.

The qualities are defined below:

- *Availability* is a measure of whether a system is there when it is needed, and whether it delivers the defined service to the agreed service levels
- *Usability* is a measure of whether customers or users are able to carry out specific tasks effectively, efficiently and with satisfaction

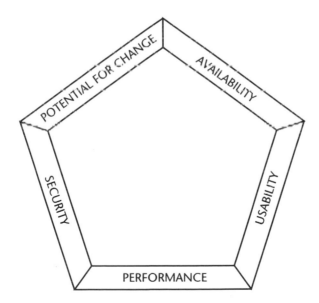

Figure 4.2 The qualities

- *Performance* is a measure of the rate at which a system is able to perform useful work and the responsiveness with which the results are presented
- *Security* is a measure of a system's ability to respond to a threat
- *Potential for change* is a measure of a system's ability, in the future, to retain or increase its value to an enterprise.

These same qualities can be used to quantify goals for all elements of the architecture. For example, when modelling the business elements, you can use availability to help assess whether the institution is providing services that its students need, when they need them, at a price that is acceptable. When modelling social system elements, availability can be a useful measure of where and when the institution is open for business and how service to students is maintained. This could prompt you to look at the impact of staff being absent through holidays or illness, or issues such as time zones for globally dispersed students. When modelling the information system, availability usually measures whether the system is there when users need it, and whether it delivers the defined service and agreed service levels.

These same qualities can be used to quantify goals for the elements from different perspectives.

For example, when viewed by the student, the performance of a learning environment is measured by the level of their qualifications and their increased potential for employment. When viewed by the staff the performance is measured by staff and institution reputation. When viewed by enterprise managers, performance is measured by external assessment of courses, procedures, course results and finances.

To help you build a value system for your institution's learning environment using these qualities, take the lists below and extend and modify them to the needs of your institution.

Availability

From the student perspective

Availability description	Goal (examples)
Choice of subject for learning	Known in the UK as the institution with the widest choice in engineering
Choice of location	Target percentage of learning available both on and off the campus
	All off-campus activities available globally
Choice of time	Target percentage of the learning tasks setting specific times for the activity
	Support services available seven days a week, 24 hours a day
Choice of learning style	Target percentage of academic programmes offers alternative learning styles to achieve the same learning outcomes
Access for non-English-speaking student groups	Target percentage of learning vehicle is available in more than one language
Access for disabled students	Target percentage of learning vehicles made available to students with disabilities

From the trading partner perspective

Trading partner	Availability description	Goal (examples)
Funding councils	Provision of accurate management and financial information	Timely submission of information required by HEFCs
Employers	Access to appropriately qualified graduates	Achieve defined level of employment among new graduates within specified timescale
Research councils	Support of quality research	Growth in levels of research council funding
Franchised colleges	Existence of franchise arrangements	Franchising of sufficient student places to meet access goals

Usability

From the student perspective

Usability description	Goal (examples)
The environment motivates the student	Target percentage of planned learntasks are completed by the student
Opportunities to apply understanding	Target percentage of learning provides opportunities to apply the outcomes, e.g. coached practice, work placement
Opportunities to review understanding	All learning provides opportunities to review work
Effective and usable learning resources	All students know how to access the resources of the institution, understand which might help them and tailor them to their personal needs

From the trading partner perspective

Trading partner	Availability description	Goal (examples)
Employers	Consistent and mutually beneficial communication between employers and the institution	Effective employer communication channels established
Franchised colleges	Access to appropriate services and support structures in the HEI for franchised student	Satisfactory external and internal audit reports on the provision
CVCP	Effective representation of the views of the HEI within the CVCP	Attain membership of key CVCP committees
Research councils	Understanding of research council policies	Key members of HEI staff focused on policy-watch
		Quality of submission (i.e. numbers accepted)

Performance

From the student perspective

Performance description	Goal (examples)
Increased employability	Known in the UK as one of the top five institutions for a source of excellent students in engineering
Student results	In the top five in published league tables for degree award track record (in student's chosen subjects)
Assessment feedback	All learning vehicles provide timely and appropriately detailed feedback on all student assignments
Adequate learning resources	All tools will be current and in common usage in industry, and so on

From the trading partner perspective

Trading partner	Availability description	Goal (examples)
ICT suppliers	Low cost equipment procurement	Effective procurement procedures implemented
Systems integrators	Open systems compliance	Effective procurement procedures implemented
Franchised colleges	Effective access to HEI	Achieve high level of final graduation from franchised students
Research councils	Quality and timeliness of research output	Percentage of theses submitted on time
		Percentage of awards granted

Security

From the student perspective

Security description	Goal (examples)
Information and counselling	All students will have access to personal support, for example pastoral tutoring, to discuss learning objectives, problems, actions needed, finance, housing, and so on
Clear understanding of costs not covered by fees	A clear statement within a student charter
Integrity of student records	Meet security of information legislation needs
Integrity of assessment/marks	No illegitimate awards associated with the institution
Finding employment	All students will have access to help in finding employment. 80 per cent of students using this service will be helped to find employment within three months

From the trading partner perspective

Trading partner	Availability description	Goal (examples)
Funding councils	Reduction of financial dependency on funding council resources	Alternative funding maximised
Franchised colleges	Assurance of quality provision in franchised colleges	Effective QA mechanisms implemented

Potential for change

From the student perspective

Potential for change description	Goal (examples)
Flexible learning	All students will have the freedom to shape the overall learning objectives and, to choose and tailor their learning to suit their needs and preferred learning styles
Mobility of learning	All students will have the freedom to choose to take learning from other institutions while accruing appropriate credit for this learning
Student-centred learning	Smaller units of study will accommodate individual students' needs: plugging gaps where necessary and avoiding unnecessary repeated work (e.g. credited for work and life experiences)
Continuous guidance	All students will be provided with appropriate help to track their changing needs and maximise their benefit from changing services offered by the institution

From the trading partner perspective

Trading partner	Availability description	Goal (examples)
Funding councils	Flexibility of strategic approach	Strategic review process implemented
Employers	Openness to changing needs of employers	Effective employer communication maintained

What next?

This chapter has looked at the importance of viewing the learning environment from different perspectives, both internal and external to the institution. You should build on the lists of needs and issues for the various perspectives presented in this chapter in order to gain a more complete picture of the requirements placed on your learning environment.

The chapter also looked at a value system defining and quantifying the goals of a learning environment using the five OPENframework qualities. This value system was presented as a set of tables which described and suggested possible goals for the key qualities of a learning environment. You should extend and elaborate these tables to understand and subsequently assess how well people's needs are met.

The next chapter defines the key business objects in a learning environment and Chapter 6 defines the key business processes. Together they form the key elements that link the business and social systems of the architecture.

5

Business Objects

This chapter describes how to define the key business objects for your institution. You need to identify your business objects so that you know which ones are the most valuable to the business. This chapter focuses on the learning environment and its constituent parts.

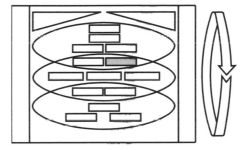

Business objects are the building blocks which are used by any of the people in the social system. For example, business objects can be quite tangible, like the PC the course developer uses to create the learning materials for students to use or, less obviously perhaps, the authoring software that runs or, is accessed by, that PC. Indeed the process of developing courseware itself could be argued to be a business object.

Business objects can be classified into two types:

- *Elemental* – an elemental business object is the lowest level of object. An example of an elemental business object is a book used by the student role in the learning process
- *Aggregated* – an aggregated business object is a higher level of object which contains lower level objects. An example of an aggregated business object is the learning environment, which is the key business object in this architecture.

This chapter defines this aggregated object of the learning environment and some of the objects it contains, many of which themselves are aggregated.

A learning environment

A learning environment is a community with its own culture and values

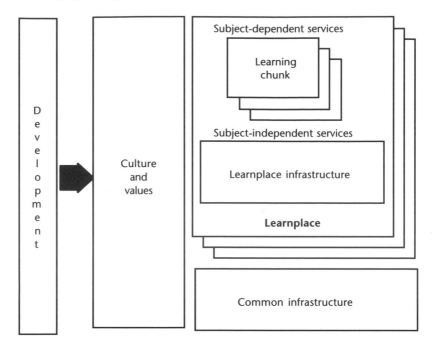

Figure 5.1 The learning environment model

providing a variety of learnplaces that support student learning (Figure 5.1). The diagram is explained on the following pages.

Learning environment culture and values

The culture of a learning environment shapes the attitudes of both staff and students. It will incorporate traditional values such as respect for differing opinions, integrity in scholarship and the pursuit of knowledge, but to be complete it also requires some less well-established values.
  These could include:

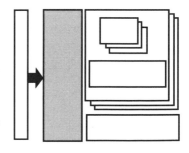

- A focus on support for student learning, rather than teaching
- Sensitivity to students' needs, for example, to individual learning styles, place of study and time constraints
- An analytic approach to the selection of knowledge media to ensure efficient and effective use of resources

- A flexibility with regards to the nature and content of learning chunks to enable penetration of new markets
- A willingness to innovate, experiment and learn from experiences elsewhere.

For students the culture could imply:

- A willingness to take responsibility for their own learning
- A recognition of the importance of study skills
- Acceptance of the notion of lifelong learning
- Use of a wide range of resources.

Cultural change is inevitably slow but can be assisted by involving staff and students in shaping changes in the learning environment.

A *learnplace*

A learnplace is a student workplace equipped to support one or more learning methods (see Chapter 6). It provides both subject-independent and subject-dependent services to the student.

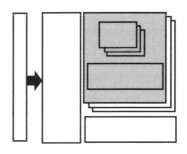

One example of a student learnplace is individual study in the library. In this example 'individual study' is the learning method and 'library' is the workplace. Another example of a student learnplace is peer learning on campus where 'peer learning' is the learning method and the campus is the student workplace. There are a number of different student workplaces which are described in more detail in Chapter 8. The set of learning methods is discussed in Chapter 6. Each institution must decide which learning methods it plans to support and at which workplaces.

Student learning at a learnplace is guided by the learning chunk (see page 57). Many learning chunks may be provided to the same learnplace. Often the same learning chunk will also be available at a number of alternative learnplaces. Sometimes a learning chunk will require the student to attend several learnplaces, for example, reading at home or in the library, lectures in lecture theatres on campus, practicals in science laboratories and TV programmes at home.

Learnplace infrastructure

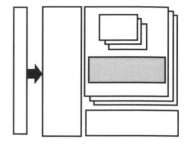

Learnplace infrastructure is a set of resources which provide services used by the student and the learning chunk at the learnplace. The resources are dedicated to the needs of the learnplace. The services provided include both subject-specific and subject-independent services.

An example of learnplace infrastructure is the set of resources required to provide the services supporting individual study in a library. These would include people in particular roles, for example the librarian or the library assistant. The learnplace infrastructure would include loan systems, ordering systems and security systems, either automated or manual. It would also include more basic resources, for example buildings, heating, plumbing and lighting.

Some infrastructure resources are oriented to the needs of a particular subject or discipline, for example language laboratories and science laboratories. This is an important point which impacts ownership and organisation of institution resources.

Once an institution has identified the set of learnplaces it plans to support, it should establish an organisation that provides the learnplace infrastructure.

Learning environment development

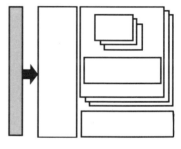

A learning environment is developed by a number of cooperating work groups both within and outside the institution.

The academic departments will lead the development of subject-specific resources while the various service departments will lead the development of the subject-independent resources.

The development of the subject-specific resources will make use of services from the learning infrastructure but will, additionally, require further development-specific resources. These are provided by the development infrastructure shown in Figure 5.2. This model shows the total infrastructure supporting the development and operation of a learning environment.

The lower portion represents the common infrastructure and the infrastructure for all learnplaces supported by the institution. We call these together the *learning infrastructure*. The learning infrastructure provides all the services required by the student. The *common infrastructure* provides services which are independent of a specific learnplace. The *learnplace infrastructure* provides services unique to a particular learnplace.

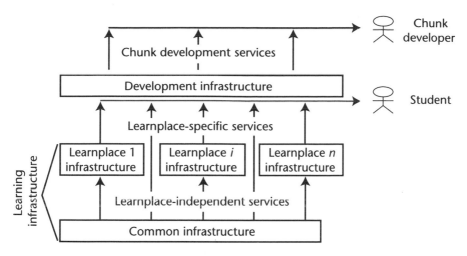

Figure 5.2 Infrastructure model

Common infrastructure

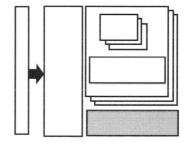

Common infrastructure is a set of resources which provide a set of services that are independent of subject and independent of learnplace. These services are used directly by the student, the learnplace infrastructure, the development infrastructure and also by the learning chunks in order to provide subject-specific services.

Many of the resources are interdependent, providing services to be used by each other in addition to their use by the student. In order to manage these complex interdependencies it is useful to organise the resources into resource layers where higher layers are dependent on the lower layers but not vice versa.

A model showing the composition of the infrastructure with the interdependencies simplified by layering is shown in Figure 5.3.

Each layer contains a number of resources. The number of layers and the content of each layer is determined by the institution. Responsibility for one or more of these resources is assigned to an institution service department. An example is given in Figure 5.4. In this example layers 1–3 represent the common infrastructure. The first layer provides services to maintain the buildings, heating, lighting, plumbing, cleaning and so on. The second layer provides services to manage the financial resources, etc. of the institution. This layer will require services from layer 1 to house the finance departments, etc. This example assumes that the resources of layer 1 are directly employed by the institution and so require human resource management. If, instead,

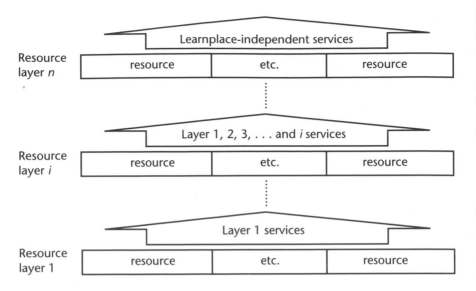

Figure 5.3 Common infrastructure model

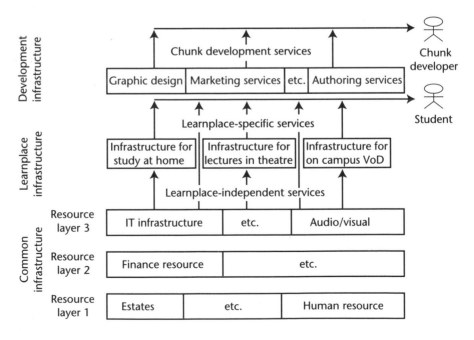

Figure 5.4 Infrastructure example

these services were outsourced, then the human resource management function could be moved up to layer 2. Layer 3 provides IT infrastructure and audio/visual services. This layer requires the services from both layers 1 and 2. In a real example more resources will exist in each layer and there will be more layers in the common infrastructure.

The example also shows the learnplace infrastructure and the development infrastructure. Resources in the development infrastructure would include computer-assisted learning (CAL) support. This resource will call on services from all layers because they need pay and accommodation. They also need to be developed as a key human resource, and will require IT infrastructure and audio/visual services, for example.

Learning chunk

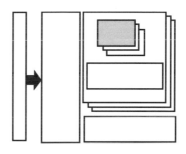

At the minimum level a learning chunk is a bounded learning activity with a specified set of learning objectives and a set of assessment procedures capable of testing to what extent these outcomes are met by students.

For the same set of learning objectives a number of learning chunks may be defined to provide additional flexibility to meet the disparate needs of different student groups and learning styles.

Multiple learning vehicles allow the HEI to offer varied products and meet individual student needs more successfully. Students have different preferences with regards to modes of learning, and the prior learning experiences of each student will dictate a different approach. The more flexibility and choice an institution is able to offer, the more widespread its appeal will be to current and potential students.

Offering a number of learning chunks provides alternative ways to meet the learning chunk objectives. The student will generally choose a single one of these but may be offered the flexibility to build his or her own set to meet personal time and place constraints, and also accommodating a preferred learning style. Where the learning chunk development team see a need to provide additional support and guidance for student learning (as will commonly be the case in undergraduate level work), they will construct or alter one or more learning vehicles. The more choice given, the higher the potential attractiveness of the course – but this will lead to higher development and delivery costs for the institution.

Learning chunks directly available to students will also include a marketing plan, fee options, syllabus and credit information. Those intended as building-blocks to larger chunks may omit these parts.

Learning chunks supporting directed learning will also include a learning vehicle to guide the learning activity more closely.

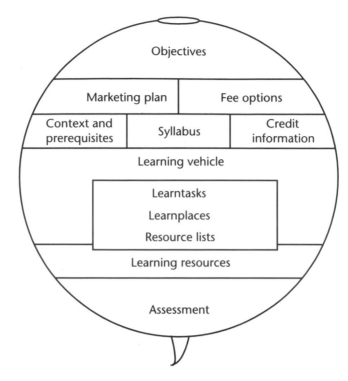

Figure 5.5 Learning chunk gooseberry model

The academic staff of departments in HEIs have many various ways of sup-porting student learning. To draw out the essence of what they do we identify the key mandatory elements, namely their objectives and assessment. For some forms of learning (for example those associated with project work or student-led investigations) these elements of a learning chunk will prove suf-ficient. For more directed learning, the learning chunk includes additional elements which are intended to guide the learning activity more closely.

To represent this large degree of flexibility in the construction of a learn-ing chunk we model it (in Figure 5.5) as a gooseberry with a hard (manda-tory) top and tail (objectives and assessment), and soft (variable) flesh that will vary from course to course and possibly from student to student. These constituent parts are described in more detail above.

Objectives
A statement of the objectives for the learning chunk should clearly state learning outcomes. Objectives, together with assessment procedures, are the only mandatory parts of a learning chunk so they need to be sufficiently detailed to enable students to construct their own learning vehicles should they so desire.

The assessment procedures would be normally defined at the same time as the learning objectives and outcomes to ensure a close correspondence.

Marketing plan

A marketing plan should make an assessment of the need for the learning chunk and describe the approach to be taken to reach identified potential student groups. It needs to cover marketing to students currently studying in the institution as well as to potential new students. The marketing materials will explain how the learning chunk relates to other learning chunks offered by the HEI and others and will identify any pre-requisites.

Fee options

This refers to a statement of fees charged to each category of students. The fee levels and arrangements for collection are likely to vary according to both the nature of the learning chunk and the category of student. Full-time students will usually pay an annual fee entitling them to study either an unlimited number or a set number of learning chunks. Part-time students on the other hand are more likely to pay on a per learning chunk basis. Information on grants and subsidies will also be included if appropriate. This fee element will be particularly important with learning chunks that are to be associated with credit accumulation and transfer schemes (CATS).

Context and prerequisites

This defines entry requirements prerequisite for specific learning chunks. Where a learning chunk is part of a logically connected course of study this will be described. It will be common for learning chunks to be designed in such a way that they form components of multiple courses.

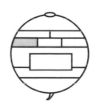

Syllabus

A syllabus is a full description of the content of the learning chunk as delivered by the learning vehicle. The syllabus will refer both to the learning chunk objectives and the assessment procedures.

Credit information

This is a statement of the credit offered on successful completion (CATS points). The CAT scheme, or its equivalent, enables comparison between learning chunks (including a rating for level) and transferability of all completed learning chunks.

Learning vehicles

Learning vehicles are a set of learning resources designed to enable students to meet the objectives of the learning chunk. Learning chunks will have only one learning vehicle, though with a variety of learning approaches included within it.

Each learning vehicle identifies a set of complementary learntasks, learnplaces and learning resource lists which together help the student meet the learning chunk objectives and successfully accomplish the assessment tasks.

A learntask is a student learning activity. A learntask is the focal part of a learning vehicle, in that its definition shapes what students actually do in the process of their learning activity. A formative assessment task is one example of a learntask. There are also non-assessed learntasks, for example group project work or individual project work. Their key characteristic is that they promote active participation of the student. Learntask definitions are written in language which may include a physical description, but should include a cognitive description of what students will do. (For example the student will practise manipulating the zoom control in order to compile the procedures for zooming in and zooming out.)

Learntask definitions may be either explicit or implicit. Explicit definitions are instructions given directly to the student through a learning resource (e.g. a worksheet taking the student through the steps of a calculation). Implicit definitions are mediated by a learning resource, (e.g. by a simulation program which leads the student from one cognitive activity to another).

Some learntasks are complex or difficult enough to warrant providing the student with interactive feedback and/or other forms of interactive support. Such support may be provided by a person (e.g. a peer, a lecturer, a mentor, a teaching assistant) or by a learning resource (e.g. an interactive computer program).

Learning vehicles, then, can have a number of relationships to learntasks. A learning vehicle may primarily serve as a way of letting the student know what the learntask consists of (e.g. goal setting); or it may serve as a form of interactive support (e.g. in giving feedback on progress or help when an impasse is reached); or it may have a more passive informational function (e.g. as a repository of 'content' or subject matter). It may combine these.

A learnplace is a student workplace equipped to support a particular learning method. It has three parts: student workplace, learning method and service provision mechanism (see page 53).

A resource list is a set of learning resources particular to a specific learning vehicle. Examples here would include reading lists, teacher-led events like lectures, tutorials and seminars, and support structures.

Learning resources

This is a statement of resources required. These may be institution-provided (library resources, online facilities, meeting space, etc.) or they may be for the student to supply (computer, books, study space, etc.). It is essential that resource provision within the HEI is closely matched to learning chunk resource requirements.

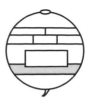

A learning resource is any resource used to support student learning, for example:

- Verbal or written guidance from academic staff
- Learning materials, for example books, articles, videos, computer-aided learning packages
- Interaction with peers and predecessors
- Prior knowledge and learning skills
- Tools such as word processors, spreadsheets, lab equipment.

For each resource alternative learnplaces may be offered, for example live and recorded lectures, real or virtual laboratories. When the resource is time constrained, temporal availability – such as stop and start dates or periodic availability – may be specified.

These different learning resources may be classified to form a hierarchy of types. This helps clarify what we mean by a learning resource and provides a tool which can be used to build a more complete picture of the learning resources in your institution.

Figure 5.6 indicates some examples of the types to be found in this hierarchy.

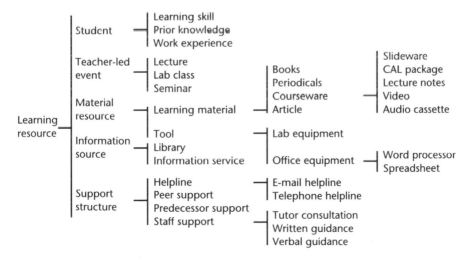

Figure 5.6 Learning resource classification tree

Assessment

This refers to one or more procedures for assessing student performance on the learning chunk, together with sample assessment materials. These may be conventional in nature (exam, written coursework) or innovative (computer-assisted assessment, peer group assessment). In some cases a student may without further study already meet the defined
objectives for a learning chunk, in which case, provided the study has not previously been assessed, there should be no objection to the student being assessed without following a formal course of study.

Relationships between chunks

It would be theoretically possible to have a learning chunk that is very small, or really quite large, for example about a third of a year of an undergraduate course. Considerations on this are that the smaller the chunk, the greater the complexity of the relationship between chunks, but this gives increased flexibility. Conversely, the bigger the chunk, the more simple the external interfaces, but the greater the complexity of the chunk itself.

The fact that chunks can, in principle, represent very small and very large learning activities has a number of implications for how we might deal with familiar educational design issues, such as relationships between aims and objectives or patterns of assessment:

- Aims and objectives – aims could be represented *within* what we have labelled the mandatory objectives part of a large chunk. That is, the definition of objectives for the chunk would be written as a hierarchical structure of general aims which are then rendered as specific objectives. Using smaller chunks, aims would be represented as a pattern of relationships *between* chunks with cognate objectives
- Context and prerequisites – this part of the chunk will logically contain the links or pointers expressing these relationships
- Assessment – similarly, one can deal with the issue of integrating assessment tasks by conceiving of large chunks covering a coherent area or a pattern of smaller chunks which are explicitly related.

What next?

This chapter has discussed the modelling of business objects. It has identified the key objects in a learning environment.

One of the key objects identified has been the learning chunk. This is a term which many may find over-colloquial, indeed we have had some difficulty with it. However, we have been at pains to avoid terms currently in use, like module, unit or course so that we could hopefully help our readers to avoid applying preconceptions in coming to grips with our definition.

You will need to tailor the definitions of the key business objects discussed in this chapter to your own needs and you should expect to add more detail to the models provided.

It is likely that you will identify new business objects as you both review and develop your business processes, or introduce new ones. For example, while you consider how you manage the interrelated development activities you will identify the need for planning documents and dependency controls.

Conversely, you can identify new processes by considering operations to be performed on the business objects. For example, operations on a learning chunk would include: create, modify, withdraw, evaluate, etc. Each operation implies the need for a process.

In the next chapter we look at the key business processes that exist in a learning environment and suggest process models for these. As you might expect, the business objects we have described in this chapter are constantly referred to in this next chapter.

6

Business Processes

This chapter discusses the development of business processes and their continuing alignment to business, social and technical systems.

As Chapter 2 described, most institutions are contemplating major changes. To accommodate change, an institution needs to examine its business processes and working practices to ensure they match the new requirements.

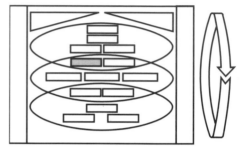

This chapter discusses the business processes of a generic HEI. It provides examples of key processes required in the management and development of learning environments for the institution. Each institution should develop its own set of business process models by extension of the examples provided here.

The process models are best represented graphically. They show relationships between processes, business objects, roles and workgroups. The graphical notation used depends on the level of the model and the purpose of the modelling.

At the highest levels the relationship between the key business objects and the key business processes is of prime interest. A notation identifying processes as boxes related by lines depicting business object flows is most useful. An example of this type of model is shown in Figure 6.1.

At even lower levels, in addition to representing the processes, objects and roles/workgroups, we also need to represent the events which trigger a process and the choices there may be between alternative actions. In this way we model an answer to the question: 'Who does what to what and when?'

- *Who* – role/workgroup
- *Does what* – process
- *To what* – object
- *When* – event/choice.

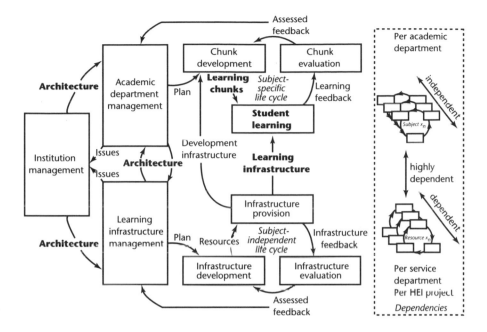

Figure 6.1 Developing and managing learning environments

Developing and managing learning environments

Figure 6.1 identifies the key processes involved in managing and developing learning environments for an institution. This model is not intended to be an exact representation of the day-to-day operations of a real institution, but we believe it captures the essential processes involved in the development and management of learning environments and their interrelationships. The notions of a flexible, reusable learning chunk and the coordinated management and development of the learning infrastructure as a core asset are not, in general, current practice. These are proposed as important aspects in the learning environment of the future.

The model shows:

- Two separate development, operation and evaluation life cycle processes: the subject-independent and the subject-dependent life cycles
- The core business process, student learning, at their intersection
- Academic departments managed independently
- Learning infrastructure managed as a core institution process to coordinate the many dependencies, both between the service departments and between the service and academic departments

- The architecture as the key output from the management processes, forming a framework for communication to coordinate the many distributed management processes
- The learning infrastructure as the key output from the subject-independent life cycle
- Learning chunks as the key output from the subject-dependent life cycle.

It is recognised that, although regarding themselves as primarily independent, dependencies do also exist between the academic departments and, indeed, that opportunities for further cooperation should be sought to increase quality and reduce costs through greater reuse.

The importance of these many dependencies cannot be overemphasised. They are represented in Figure 6.1 by the dependencies box on the right-hand side of the diagram. Mechanisms for managing these dependencies include the communication of architecture, plans, issues and feedback. These are discussed briefly in the management section below. The process models you construct to represent your institution should decompose and extend as necessary to ensure that all these dependencies are fully understood.

Some of the terms used within this and later chapters maintain a division of responsibilities traditional to the sector, and especially that between academic and service staff and structures. These divisions are blurring: in some institutions curriculum delivery, traditionally reserved for academic staff, now involves learning support staff; some aspects of service support are migrating to academic departments. The most sensible form of analysis is thus to tease out key business processes and then the processes needed to support these. Each institution will then derive a structure most appropriate to its circumstances; this may or may not represent the conventional division of labour.

Please refer to Chapter 4 for further discussion of the institution architecture and Chapter 5 for further discussion of the learning infrastructure and learning chunks.

Management

The management processes are meant to ensure that the quality of student learning is maximised while the institution meets its financial and other constraints.

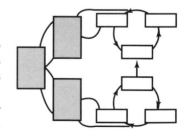

A key output from the institution management process is an architecture which expresses the institution's vision, values, objectives and its strategies for implementation and the management of change.

This overall institution architecture will define the organisation and assign ownership for the more detailed parts of the architecture to the different departments. These departments will develop their parts within the framework defined by the institution architecture.

It is the management process which is responsible for setting direction, prioritising activities, securing resources, planning implementation and monitoring progress. The institution management process will set the direction for the institution and establish an organisation capable of meeting its mission. This will be documented in the institution's architecture, supported as necessary by detailed organisation definitions, budget allocations and so on.

The architecture will allocate responsibility for different sections to the respective service departments. For example, a central IT services department may be empowered to define the section related to IT provision for the institution including, for example, its processes, roles and trading relationships. This forms a part of the overall architecture and becomes an essential mechanism for communication through the institution to align its interdependent activities. Each service department will, either individually or in cooperation with other service departments, implement mechanisms and create relationships to ensure that the needs of the academic departments are:

• Understood (see architecture feedback loop in the model)
• Implementable (see issues feedback loop in the model)
• Continuously monitored (infrastructure evaluation and feedback in the model).

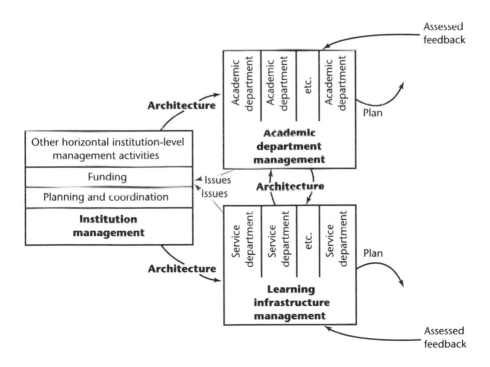

Figure 6.2 Management process model

The different academic departments will, in general, adapt this total architecture for their own use. We recommend that each department define its own architecture in terms of its usage of the institution's infrastructure services. It may be appropriate to define discipline-level architectures rather than department-level architectures where commonality across departments within a discipline is large.

The management process model is shown in Figure 6.2. The horizontal, institution-wide, management processes are described in more detail below.

Planning and coordination

This process identifies the needs of the learning environment based on analysis of its business processes. This will include analysis of the actual processes which will be found through feedback mechanisms from the various departments in addition to analysis of current and proposed business processes which are modelled in the architecture. The result of this analysis will be a prioritised list of learning resource development activities with nominated responsibility. This list can then be converted into a plan by allocation of funded development activities divided into costed achievable tasks with start and end dates and any possible interdependencies marked. Coordination of these development activities involves monitoring progress of the separate development tasks so that these interdependencies are carefully managed.

The planning processes can be achieved using a number of well-established project management methods. The analysis phase may use one or more of the following approaches:

- Bottom-up, participatory, by committee
- Top-down, directive, by individual
- External, by consultant.

A further extract from the JISC *Guidelines for Developing an Information Strategy* may be worth considering at this point:

> The process . . . suggests that the production of an Information Strategy in an HEI is more complex than in almost all other organisations; this is because while, in one sense an HEI needs to act in a 'business-like' manner, in fact most behave like loosely connected, anarchic groups of dedicated individuals. Thus any attempt to develop a set of attitudes simply by a top-down, hierarchically driven process is doomed to failure. The process must also have a bottom-up analysis. But not in isolation: each institution needs some overall sense of its direction and some sense of coherence amongst the people *who work there.*
>
> (JISC 1995b: 15)

Funding

HEIs obtain their primary funding for teaching and learning from five sources:

- The appropriate higher education funding council
- local authority fees
- research councils
- Self-funded overseas and EU students (full and part-time)
- Overseas students fee income.

The block grant obtained from the funding council is calculated on the basis of the student numbers allocated to that institution, having regard to the funding council's view of the notional cost of each student in relation to the discipline they are studying. The allocations take further account of the research rating within the institution. The fee income from local authorities is automatic for those home students who have been accepted by the institution.

It is not a requirement of the institution to then allocate this funding to disciplines on the same basis that it was calculated. Every institution has the right to take its own view about the allocation of the block grant. Full cost fees are chargeable to overseas students and may be used without restriction. Research council grants, however, are specific to the student and the course of study and must be used accordingly.

Funding for the learning environment must be split between the various departments. The infrastructure provided by the subject-independent life cycle is used by most of the academic departments but not equally. Three alternatives for funding these shared services are possible:

- Top-sliced funding for all services
- Budget totally devolved to academic departments who are charged for infrastructure services
- A combination of these with top-sliced funding for core services and charging for others.

Subject-specific life cycle

The subject-specific life cycle delivers chunks to the student learning process and monitors the quality of the learning experience provided for its students.

Learning experience feedback gathered in this way is analysed and opportunities for improvement identified and communicated to the appropriate planning or development process.

Each academic department operates this life cycle independently. Each department is responsible for development, provision to student learning and evaluation of its own set of chunks. Each department is, however, highly dependent on the many departments responsible for providing learning infrastructure.

These dependencies should as far as possible be anticipated and detailed in the institution architecture. The architecture should also ensure that mechanisms are created which provide visibility of and feedback opportunity to plans to develop infrastructure resources. What form these mechanisms take is an institution decision but possibilities include organisational structure, committee management and IT-assisted group working.

Subject-independent life cycle

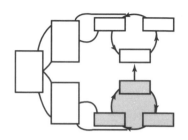

The subject-independent life cycle delivers learning infrastructure resources, which are not subject-specific, to the student learning process.

The life cycle should develop the required resources to an agreed specification which is monitored by the infrastructure provision process. Generated feedback is evaluated and used to steer future developments. For example this could be achieved through service level agreements or by a partnership model.

Each service department is responsible for operating this life cycle. The number and types of service departments are matters for each institution. However, examples would include the library, IT service department, CAL support group, estates department, audio/visual service department and so on. In general, they are dependent on one another. A library, for example, would require buildings, heating, lighting, plumbing, IT and so on. It would, therefore, need to liaise with these other service departments in order that it could meet its own service level agreement. Service departments are also highly dependent on the academic departments, for example a library needs to stock books required by learning chunks currently offered to its students. These dependencies necessitate coordinated planning of the learning environment as detailed above in the management section. Output from these processes are sets of plans which drive this life cycle process.

Student learning

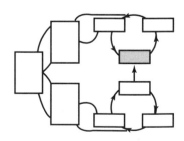

The student learning process provides a learning environment for the student, giving access to the appropriate resources from the institution's learning infrastructure, helping them identify the most suitable learning styles for themselves and supplying them with tailorable learning chunks to match these styles (see Figure 6.3).

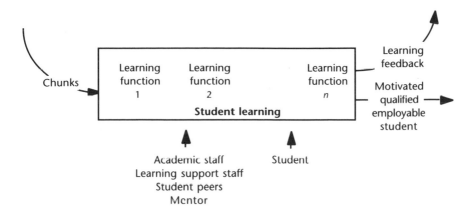

Figure 6.3 The student learning process

Its key output is a stream of students motivated to be lifelong learners with recognised qualifications and increased prospects of employment.

The primary input to this process is the learning chunk from the subject-specific life cycle supported by learning infrastructure from the subject-independent life cycle. Outputs include learning feedback which is evidence to be used to evaluate the quality of the student learning process. Student work, for example essays and project reports, is often used as a part of learning feedback.

The student learning process itself may be split into a number of sub-processes called learning functions. The number and definition of each of these functions depends on the purpose for decomposition. They should, however, be mutually independent and together cover all the parts of student learning. We offer three such decompositions in Appendix C. The process is carried out by the student role, guided by academic staff and reinforced by the student's peers.

A successful learning vehicle will provide all these functions through its learntasks and learning resources. It is useful to look at the current methods of implementing these functions to illustrate how these methods can be mapped to the functions to help quantify the quality of a particular method.

One classification of such learning methods is shown in Table 6.1 in the left column. These learning methods are mapped to the fundamental learning functions indicating their effectiveness.

Table 6.1 shows that each learning method is better at providing some learning functions than others. A successful learning vehicle provides for all the functions. These learning functions are more fully defined in Appendix C.

Using this mapping technique you can assess the completeness of your learning vehicles. You may extend or replace the set of methods and you may choose an alternative set of learning functions to suit best the needs of your

Table 6.1 Learning methods, effectiveness of learning functions

Learning methods	Learning functions					
	Orientation	*Motivation*	*Presentation*	*Clarification*	*Elaboration*	*Confirmation*
Lecture	Low	Medium	High	Low	Low	Low
Tutorial	Medium	Medium	Low	High	High	Medium
Seminar	Medium	Medium	Medium	High	High	Medium
Practical	Low	Medium	Low	Medium	High	High
Assessment	Medium	Medium	Low	Medium	Low	High
Coaching	High	High	Medium	Medium	Medium	Medium
Peer	Medium	Medium	Low	Medium	Medium	Medium
Individual	Medium	Medium	Low	Medium	Medium	High

institution. It is important, however, that your set of methods be carried forward when you identify your set of learnplaces since the methods form the link between learning functions and learnplaces.

Figure 6.4 shows that a learning method provides some but not all of the learning functions and that it is supported at a number of learnplaces. For further information about learnplaces refer to Chapter 8.

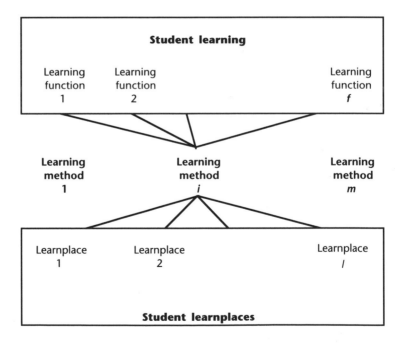

Figure 6.4 Learning methods link functions and learnplaces

It will be necessary to look at traditional learning methods in the light of the changing requirements, but not necessarily with a view to discarding them altogether.

To take one small but pivotal example, the question, what media of communication can best partially or wholly replace 'live' lectures, is at the centre of pressure of innovation. Lectures are great constrainers of time and place. There are answers to this question in terms of the lecture as an information process – its powers to inform, to motivate, elaborate or to confirm understanding. But there are also issues about the 'unwritten' curriculum that is conveyed in lecturing – all the nuances about what is 'really important', where the 'official position' is perhaps not to be taken too literally, what motivates the researchers who reveal this knowledge, what is controversial and what is routine, and what is expected of the student in terms of implicit grasp of the 'game' – right down to whether they get the jokes. There is also all the social experience of sitting through lectures with fellow students, observing their reactions, misunderstandings and feelings about the lectures.

It is an enduring puzzle to many lecturers why lectures continue to persist as a medium of teaching. In many areas excellent published lectures exist, in media capable of freeing the student in time and space. Some of the reasons for lectures' failure to die lie in their information transmission properties, but others lie in the social setting. Which social processes can be supported by different media of lecture transmission, and how these change the result are questions right at the centre of current innovation. The HEI that understands these issues for its students in its context will succeed in innovation; the one that fails to understand them will fail. We need not be pessimistic that the live lecture is irreplaceable. Some studies have shown alternatives to be superior (in some contexts and for some purposes) but a principled understanding of the social changes wrought by the new media lies at the heart of successful innovation.

Learning to learn

Learning to learn can be regarded as both another form of subprocess and as an output (part of being a learned student). As HEIs adopt a student-centred approach to the development of learning environments and offer students more choice in how they implement the learning process, they will have to help students learn how to make best use of the resources and opportunities available – they will have to help them 'learn to learn'.

The learning-to-learn subprocess will need to make full and explicit information on courses available to students and prospective students for two important reasons: to help pre-students make their choices, and (on an ongoing basis from time of enrolment onwards) to facilitate sensible decisions as to when and where to learn, what resources students will need, what resources will be made available to them, and what is expected of them.

Consideration will also have to be given to informing tutors, learning managers and mentors, because counselling and guidance is an important aspect of learning to learn.

One approach would be to make a set of guides available to cover, for example:

* Students – student guide and assessment guide
* Tutors – tutor guide
* Workplace – mentor guide.

The following examples of guides are taken from Freeman and Lewis (1995), *Writing Open Learning Materials*.

Checklist of components and possible contents

The following list shows possible contents of differing supplementary materials. These are offered only as ideas – content will vary depending on:

* The learners and other users for whom the material is designed
* The curriculum area
* The extent of the course
* The method of delivery of the course
* The other materials used in the course.

Some overlap between components will often occur, for example a tutor guide may include material from a student guide, slightly adapted.

Student guide
* Overall aims, objectives/outcomes of the course and where each is covered
* Structure of the course and possible routes through it
* Overview of course components and their purposes
* How to get the most out of each component of the course
* Any prerequisites – what the student needs to know or be able to do before starting the course
* Services to which the student is entitled, for example contacts with a tutor
* Advice on how to study, for example how to prepare for assignments, time management
* Advice on how to set up self-help groups
* Useful contacts – names, addresses, telephone numbers, details of how and when contact can be made
* Glossary/index
* Feedback form on the guide.

Assessment guide
* Overview of the assessment scheme for the course – what is assessed, when, where, how and by whom
* Links between learning outcomes and assessment – student capacities and competences to be assessed

- Number of assessments and their nature
- Types of assessment, for example report, case study, presentation
- Any course assessment weighting, and how the overall grade/mark/result is calculated
- Explanation of the grading scheme
- The assignments themselves, with dates for submission
- Information on how marks are allocated within each assignment
- Guidelines on how to answer assignments – in general and for each separate assignment
- Advice on action to take if dissatisfied with a mark/grade, the appeals procedure, any regulations
- Feedback form on the guide.

Tutor guide
- Overview of course materials and content (see many items in the student guide heading)
- The role of the tutor in the scheme – what the tutor does, how and when
- Contacts with the student – post, face to face, telephone, other
- Overview of assessment (see items on the assessment guide)
- Notes on marking assignments, both general and for each assignment
- Examples of typical student answers and how a tutor might respond to each
- Outlines of tutorials – content and set-up arrangements
- Record keeping
- Typical student queries and how to respond
- Tutor briefing and training arrangements
- Tutoring styles and standards
- Monitoring and evaluation of tutors
- Feedback form on the guide.

Workplace mentor guide
- Outline of the course, its components and the purposes of each
- Who does what – for example, the student, the tutor, the administrator
- Links with the workplace
- Benefits to the line manager
- What the line manager can do to help, how and when
- Who to contact for more information
- Feedback form on the guide.

The development of the learning-to-learn process is a major project at the University of Humberside, where they are developing a computer-based system to support it. With their permission, we describe it in Figure 6.5 as a useful example of the things that need to be taken into account.

Introduction – this tells the student about learning to learn, why it will be useful to them and what it involves. It sets it in the context of the HEI's mission and shows how it will contribute to lifelong learning.

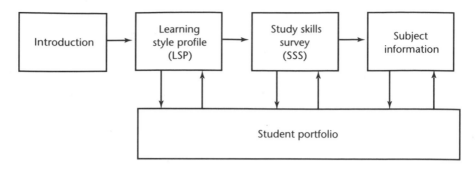

Figure 6.5 The learning-to-learn system

Learning style profile (LSP) – this module is based on a tool created by Honey and Mumford (1992), which is widely used for management development by industry. It is based on the premise that everyone has their own preferred learning style, though this can be greatly affected by context, and it is recognised that people may use different learning styles in different contexts. The profile outlines four broad-based categories and measures the degree to which an individual fits each of these learning styles, thus building up a learning profile for the individual.

This module offers students the following benefits:

- It demonstrates that different people learn in different ways, which can help the student understand how different types of learning situation can affect achievement
- It makes them more aware of situations in which they can learn more effectively, and those in which they do not
- It helps them develop their own learning styles and so become more effective learners.

Once students have worked through the LSP and collected a printout of their results, they will be helped to construct an action plan. This will consist of activities they can undertake to develop their learning styles and thus, the effectiveness of their learning.

Students' results are stored in a database, each student having access to their own. It is intended to use the data amassed for further research.

Study skills survey (SSS) – once students have used the LSP to consider their preferred learning styles, they move on to the study skills survey. This module identifies study skills, the key skills students need to successfully complete their programme of study. These include:

- Attitude to study and learning
- Time management
- Note taking
- Collecting information.

For each of the skills identified each student is asked to complete a series of questions on their attitude towards it, and their current practice in that area. This builds up a profile for that student in each skill area and highlights those they need to develop further.

At this stage attitudes to study are measured, rather than capability in each area of study. Tests for capability on specific skills, such as numeracy and IT, occur later in the programme, in subject information.

Like LSP, the student is assisted in the development of an SSS action plan.

Subject information – the fourth element of the model is subject information. This will make full use of the university computer network to provide a flexible information system, capable of giving uniquely personal and appropriate information to each student. The system will draw upon data from students' own 'accounts' detailing the units of study they are taking, and from central, comprehensive information about each study unit, covering the kind of detail outlined earlier in this chapter.

To consolidate the learning from this experience, and to make sure that the students make use of the information they have gained, they will be asked to continue to develop their own portfolio comprising:

- LSP action plan
- SSS action plan
- Programme of generic skills study for the next semester.

The portfolio will provide students with a focus for reflection on learning to learn and a tangible way of demonstrating they have completed it. It will also stimulate dialogue between students and their tutors. Generic skills modules include:

- Study skills
- Asking research questions
- Group skills
- Presentation skills
- Media skills
- Basic numeracy
- Report writing
- Dissertation skills
- Writing skills (in multimedia form)
- Tutorials/guides on IT.

Learning to learn will help students manage their own learning. It will also develop students as independent and lifelong learners by making effective use of their own time, tutors and other support staff, learning materials and technology. It will inform and guide tutorial contact with students. The process is supportive of all HEI learning environments.

Chunk development

The chunk development process provides learning chunks for the student learning process. The structuring of students' activity is the prime focus.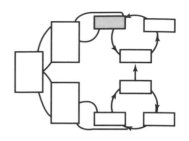

The development subprocesses follow a general plan, analyse, design and implement pattern applied to the parts of a learning chunk.

The plan generated by the academic department's management process identifies the need for particular new or enhanced learning chunks. This department plan communicates the requirement, budget and timescales for a set of chunk development projects. This is shown in Figure 6.6, which illustrates the internal subprocesses of chunk development and its relationship with the subject-specific life cycle and the management processes. Notice that the assessed feedback from chunk evaluation influences the chunk development process. This feedback is input to the plan process which schedules appropriate analysis, design and implementation activities.

The process outputs learning chunks to the student learning process. The subprocesses of chunk development are presented in more detail below.

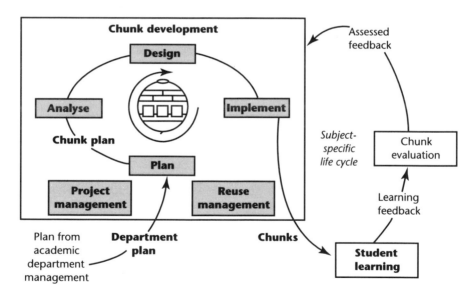

Figure 6.6 The chunk development process

Plan

This process establishes a chunk development plan based on the learning chunk requirement in the department plan. This chunk development plan drives all subsequent development stages. It may be modified due to changing circumstances by the project management process.

The planning process considers the budget, content and timescale requirements and produces a chunk development plan which satisfies these. If this is not possible it is raised as an issue to the academic department management process.

All parts of the gooseberry model (see Chapter 5) must be considered and development activities planned to ensure their completion. For example:

- The learning chunk's objectives and assessment methods – these should be defined first and should elaborate the content requirements in the department plan
- The learning chunk's marketing plan – the target group(s) for the learning chunk should be defined. Promotional channels should be identified or their development planned
- The learntasks and learning resources – the key sources of information should be identified in the plan. These could be people or information services.

All development resources must be identified and coordination of their activities planned. For example:

- Agree learnplaces to be supported. These identify student workplaces and service provision mechanisms including media for learning resources, etc.
- Identify needs for specialist skills or knowledge; secure and schedule their involvement
- Capture the interdependencies and ensure adequate communication between all players.

All opportunities for reuse should be identified and clarified in the plan. For example:

- Consider the relationship between this learning chunk and other learning chunks; this may lead to increased sharing of learning resources between the learning chunks
- Scan for reuse opportunities at all stages: planning, analysis, design and implementation
- Scan for reuse opportunities from many sources: at local development team level, within department, at institution across departments level, across institutions, to national initiatives and international initiatives
- Increase the opportunity for subsequent reuse by planning the development of reusable learning chunks and reusable learning chunk parts.

Analyse

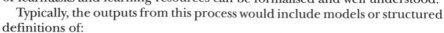

This process creates a thorough description of the learning
chunk and its context so that the requirements for the design
of learntasks and learning resources can be formalised and well understood.

Typically, the outputs from this process would include models or structured
definitions of:

- The target student users, both as individuals and in workgroups
- The learnplaces, including specification of student workplaces and service
  provision mechanisms including media for learning resources, etc.
- The learntasks
- Clustering of learntasks and learning resources into appropriate categories
  to increase the potential for subsequent reuse.

Inputs to this process come from the world of work – as new working practices evolve, new standards of vocational competence are set, and new sets of
skills and knowledge are recognised and articulated; also from the world of
academic research, with the growth of research-based knowledge and changing views about what students should come to know.

Most of the changes in work-based and research-based definitions of worthwhile learning are incremental, but sometimes the shift is radical, e.g. where
IT automates a set of business processes, or a new combination of disciplines
emerges.

Design

This process defines the learntasks and creates an external
view of a chunk's learning resources and their associated
parts. Typically, the outputs from this process would include:

- Collaboration mechanisms to support information interchange between
  the various groups involved in chunk development, for example compati-
  ble word processing formats
- Templates to communicate design detail and to formalise rules for presentation
- Existing learning chunks or learning chunk parts found by searching existing learning resource repositories which can be reused by this learning
  chunk
- Prototype implementation mock-ups to demonstrate design standards and
  ideas.

Implement

This process outputs a complete and tested learning chunk
that is ready for student use in the institution's learning

environment. It also becomes a potentially reusable asset in the subsequent development of other learning chunks.

While, occasionally, the implementation of a learning chunk might necessitate the creation of all brand new learning resources, this is unusual. Generally, most learning resources are acquired and possibly modified, and others are newly implemented. These learning resources are then integrated as required to form the learning vehicle for the learning chunk.

Tasks involved in the implementation process include:

- Creating top level structures and models – these may be developed specifically for a package or alternatively as reusable tools in the implementation process
- Defining models – top level models and structures are detailed to further define learning vehicle information
- Integrating media – the media elements such as video and sound are transformed into a format suitable for the learning package, e.g. digitising of sound and conversion to suitable formats. The transformed media elements are then integrated into the package
- Accommodating the link with learning chunk and student assessment – for example, in computer-based vehicles this could be accomplished by using automated tools for monitoring student progress. This information could be made available only to the student, for self-assessment, or may be made more generally available for institution assessment of students and learning chunks
- Testing of the package for content, accuracy and functionality.

Project management

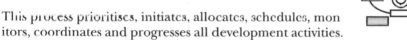

This process prioritises, initiates, allocates, schedules, monitors, coordinates and progresses all development activities.

It establishes the need for resources and estimates both time and resource to meet the target timescales. It acquires the required human and technical resources. It makes decisions balancing cost, risk and timescales, and adjusts activities accordingly.

Technical resources include:

- Design and delivery platforms
- Information capture tools
- Authoring and information processing tools.

Human resources include:

- Academic authors
- Designers
- Graphics artists
- Media producers.

The many various and specialist skills involved in a chunk development project will often require the creation of collaborations both with other departments in an institution and also outside organisations. The coordination of activities with such an organisationally and geographically dispersed team presents a large challenge which is managed by this process.

Reuse management

This process manages the availability of existing knowledge and information resources and the creation of future resources such that they are more easily assimilated into other learning chunks.

This process uses the following approaches to improve the ability to reuse these resources:

* Standardisation – agree standard formats, tools, policies
* Design for reuse – define rules, templates, methods, etc. to encourage reusable resources
* Registering – record existence of the resource with appropriate keys and links to facilitate its being found by others
* Searching – facilities to help find registered resources based on their keys or content
* Browsing – facilities to help find registered resources based on their inter-linkage
* Classification – schemes on which to build useful interlinkages between resources.

The process is concerned with resources at a number of levels:

* Within the chunk development team
* Within the department
* Between departments within an institution
* In other institutions, both in the UK and globally
* From national initiatives (e.g. Computers in Teaching Initiative and the Teaching and Learning Technology Programme)
* From international initiatives.

The knowledge and information resources made accessible by this process are used by all the subprocesses of chunk development.

Chunk evaluation

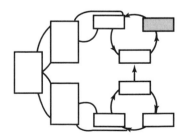

The student learning process monitors the quality of the learning experience provided for its students and provides feedback. This learning experience feedback is analysed by the chunk evaluation process, and opportunities for improvement are identified and communicated to the appropriate planning or development process.

Chunk evaluation has two main purposes: better support of student learning, and continuous realignment of learning chunk objectives with external demands (for example changing needs of industry, advances in research-based knowledge).

Supporting student learning

A learning chunk needs to be evaluated to ensure that students taking it:

- Meet the chunk objectives and learning outcomes
- Make the most effective use of their abilities and the resources provided
- Meet their individual restrictions (for example must study at home)
- Feel positive about the chunk's objectives, resources, assessment methods, etc., or conversely can initiate a process of remedying defects in the chunk.

Checking appropriateness of objectives

A learning chunk needs to be evaluated to ensure that its objectives are still appropriate. Most, if not all, learning chunks aim to increase a student's knowledge with the intention of increasing their employability. A learning chunk needs to be evaluated to ensure that students who have successfully completed it:

- Have acquired knowledge which is current, not dated
- Learn the most appropriate techniques using the most commonly employed tools
- Are able to apply the knowledge and skills acquired effectively and thus increase their employability.

Infrastructure development

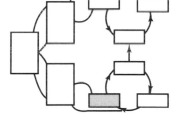

This process delivers learning infrastructure resources to the infrastructure provision process, which makes these available to the student learning and chunk development processes as a set of services.

The different resources are often grouped into service departments. Each service department is responsible for the development of its own resources.

The process of infrastructure development determines what infrastructural services are required to meet the needs of student learning, as defined and informed by the learning infrastructure management process. Infrastructural services requirements are also informed by the more precise needs of the subject-specific life cycle, which also determines broadly how these services will be provided.

The overall management processes associated with the definition of the learning environment will set the general parameters controlling the development of specific infrastructural services. It is important to recognise this dependent relationship. While service providers will no doubt be an important source of intelligence as regards new technological developments and new technological possibilities for the delivery of teaching and learning, the institutional approach should be driven not by technology but by institutional teaching and learning strategy, which should itself be governed by the vision and mission of the institution as a whole. For example, one institution may decide that focusing on traditional small-group teaching methods will better serve its institutional objectives, while another will emphasise computer-based distance learning. There is no ideal solution, only a need to ensure that the mode of delivery can be successfully supported, and that the overall pattern of delivery is consistent with institutional objectives.

In practice the institution is likely to wish to support a variety of modes of teaching and learning, and the design of infrastructural services will be influenced significantly by the subject-specific life cycle associated with chunk development, student learning and chunk evaluation. A key issue in the infrastructure design process will be the maintenance of consistency between the high-level, institutionally derived definition of necessary infrastructural services and the demands generated in the course of the subject-specific life cycle. Ideally the development process should be a consistent implementation of institutional strategy in each subject-specific context.

How this is done will differ between institutions, however; each must decide the number and types of service departments it requires and how their interdependencies will be managed. Some common examples of service department are: estates, library, staff development, IT infrastructure, audio/visual and CAL support. Within these departments will lie the responsibility for network support, library automation and user interface design, for example. These service functions may be provided by institution staff or may be outsourced or a combination of these.

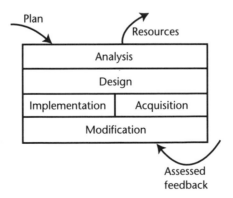

Figure 6.7 The infrastructure development model

While each service department will have its own development process, in general, it will be divided into subprocesses like Figure 6.7. Each subprocess of this general approach is described in the following sections. A single scenario is used to provide examples in each section. The scenario assumes that an IT service department is planning to provide automated chunk ordering and payment services.

Analysis

Each service department should establish the needs of the learning environment based on analysis of its business processes. Ideally, this is achieved in partnership with the management planning process (see above).

The first stage concentrates on an analysis of the kinds of infrastructural services required to meet the needs of the learning environment. It should not be concerned at this point with the mechanisms for providing these services. The questions to be considered at this stage include, for example: what information services must be provided? Will these be provided electronically? What do students and lecturers need? What are the training needs?

The outcome should be almost an inventory of service requirement driven by the overall needs of the institutional teaching and learning strategy, and developed in detail in terms of the needs of the subject-specific context. The steps involved in this analysis are described below with examples illustrating each step.

- Higher-level process models are broken into subprocesses. Process models are created for chunk selection, enrolment, ordering and payment
- Roles and workgroups supporting these processes are identified and described, for example, roles would include the student doing the enrolling, paying, etc., the administrative assistant managing enrolment, etc. Workgroups would include finance departments, student help centres, etc.
- Aggregated business objects are split into constituent parts, for example, the learning chunk may need to be split further to support chunk selection better. Analysis would aim to answer the question: on which parts of a chunk does the student base selection?
- Service requirements are established by:
  - Analysis of operations on the business objects, for example, operations on learning chunk descriptions would include create, update, delete, etc. Operations on a register of learning chunks would include add, remove, find, merge, etc.
  - Analysis of role needs, for example, a student selecting a learning chunk will require a list of learning chunks. This list would, ideally, be filtered according to personal preferences (location, learning styles, etc.), filtered according to current learning (exclude ones already done, exclude ones where prerequisites are not met, etc.).

Service requirements are elaborated by considering the workplace at which the service is to be provided, for example, IT-facilitated learning chunk selection may be provided for the student either on campus or from home or both.

Design

Based on the analysis above, each service department should design a solution which meets the service requirements. A key decision here is between implementation, acquisition and modification.

The second major stage of the development process considers how these services will be provided. This is increasingly complex as alternatives to centrally provided services at the institutional level emerge. This is in part the outcome of the decentralisation of computing which has broken down the centrality of the mainframe and empowered departmental and end-user computing. More can now be provided at local levels and this increases the choices. At the same time, there is a move away from the institution and upwards to the national level in the provision of certain kinds of services. This applies particularly to the information services being organised through the Higher Education Funding Council's Joint Information Systems Committee. At a time of rapid change, the commitment to the principle of top-slicing to support system-wide investment gives considerable strength to the HE system, but challenges institutions to think in new ways about infrastructural design. In order to help the infrastructure designer with these complex problems a stepwise approach to design is advocated. The steps involved are described below with examples illustrating each step:

- The target solution is organised into subsystems composed of social and technical system elements, for example, the subsystems could be aligned to the processes: a learning chunk selection subsystem, a learning chunk ordering subsystem, etc.
- The social system elements of each subsystem are rigorously specified, for example, the learning chunk selection process, the roles supporting it, the objects involved: learning chunk descriptions, learning chunk registers, learning chunk filtered lists, etc.
- The technical system components are rigorously specified, for example, user interface components, database components, business logic components and encapsulated legacy components specified as object types.
- The technical system components are clustered into design modules.

The designer must decide what qualities to optimise to steer design decisions. In addition to the five qualities introduced in Chapter 4, cost, risk and timescales are often important considerations.

Implementation

Implementation is guided by design and takes many forms. A change to a role or a business process may be implemented by staff training, staff recruitment or outsourcing.

The addition of a new type of student workplace may be implemented by enhancement to the institution IT infrastructure, extensions to student-provided equipment and additional information provided by helplines to support these upgrades.

The implementation may involve rethinking the relationships between existing academic services, such as the library and the computing centre. In many institutions these two services have now been merged. However, the approach advocated in this book might lead to a much more radical outcome, in which existing units are re-engineered into quite different organisational structures which correspond better to the needs of users of the learning environment.

Acquisition

Acquisition is also guided by the design. The service requirement with defined goals for each of the qualities, together with goals for cost, risk and timescales, should be used as acceptance criteria.

Each of the candidate products or services to be acquired are tested against these criteria in the selection process.

Modification

Most often change is effected by modification of the existing infrastructure – evolution rather than revolution. It is very important that the analysis and design stages are not skipped.

Tweaking the separate subsystems without regard to their interdependencies is usually very costly. You can reduce this problem by careful design which creates largely independent subsystems with well-understood boundaries and a high potential for change. It will be important to follow a specified change control procedure when implementing changes.

Infrastructure provision

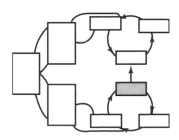

This process makes the resources output from the infrastructure development process available to the student learning and chunk development processes as a set of services. It concerns the practical operation of the outcome of the development process.

This will usually take the form of a new or enhanced resource, for example a change in the organisation, a new workplace, a new service at an existing workplace, an improved process, etc.

The different resources are often grouped into service departments who are responsible for developing and providing the services.

In terms of organisational structures, this may be achieved in a variety of ways depending on how radical a change is required. There may be a whole-sale re-engineering of the organisation of service provision or a more evolutionary approach may be taken. This in turn is likely to have an influence on the management styles adopted: hierarchical or non-hierarchical, directive or collegial.

The process of providing the infrastructure will need to be sensitive to change and to the development of new models of teaching and learning. The provision of each new workplace may require new services.

In all cases there will need to be a much more detailed analysis of the service requirements in terms of the workplaces at which the services are to be provided. This is discussed in greater detail in Chapter 8. This part of the process will also entail a more detailed specification of the service provider roles which need to be fulfilled. This is discussed at greater length in Chapter 7. Finally it will be necessary to specify the key IT and other equipment components which will be needed to support the learning environment, and to implement procedures for their procurement, installation and support. This is further discussed in Chapter 9.

Infrastructure evaluation

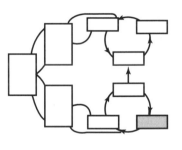

Each infrastructure provision process monitors the quality of the services delivered to its users and provides feedback. This feedback is analysed by the infrastructure evaluation process and opportunities for improvement identified and communicated to the appropriate planning or development process.

Regardless of the precise form of organisation of service provision, mechanisms for the evaluation of these services need to be embedded in the infrastructure. Operating these mechanisms should be a key management task. Once again there are a number of ways of achieving this, including the use of formal performance indicators, the development of user feedback techniques and the implementation of service level agreements. In a decentralised, non-hierarchical structure, management will have a particular responsibility for helping individual provider units to develop clear aims and objectives and for supporting them in achieving the desired outcomes.

However, evaluation should not be confined to the services themselves. The procedures whereby information from other business processes concerned with the development of the learning environment feed into the processes of infrastructure design and provision also need to be carefully monitored to ensure that they are effective. Planning the development of the learning environment and of its associated infrastructure needs to be informed by the broader process of institutional management, so that the learning environment accurately incorporates institutional aims and objectives. Formal mechanisms need to be put in place to ensure this happens, and they need to be regularly evaluated.

Input from the academic management process also needs to be formalised and managed. In most institutions this is perhaps the most difficult challenge. Using the Learning Environment Architecture should help to provide a shared understanding of the interdependency of the different processes involved in the management and development of the learning environment. It is essential to avoid any breakdown in communication between those developing new learning chunks and those responsible for service provision at the infrastructural level. The subject-specific life cycle and the subject-independent life cycle must be strongly articulated, and the mechanisms for achieving this must again be subject to regular evaluation.

What next?

This chapter presented a business process model for the development, operation and continuous improvement of a learning environment for a generic institution. It identified and described a number of the key business processes in the top-level model.

Using a similar approach you need first to identify your business processes, then evaluate how well they match your current and future business requirements and decide what changes, if any, need to be made. The model presented here provides a useful reference point. We recommend that you use it to ensure completeness of your model. However, it is unlikely that you will wish to look at all the HEI's processes at once. When you have determined what your key issues are, we recommend that you look at the processes relating to them.

These processes will be input for the definition of roles, workplaces, services and components as described in Chapters 7, 8 and 9.

7

Social System

This chapter provides a model for defining the social system. The social system describes how people are organised, how they operate and the structure that supports them. It includes a picture of the external groups with which the HEI interfaces, the organisational structure, the roles people perform, and how people with differing roles form workgroups.

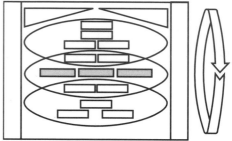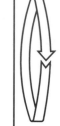

The social system is divided into the following topics:

- *People* associated with HEIs can be classified as influencers, users, service providers and related agencies
- *Organisational structure* affects both the internal and external interfaces of the HEI. The manner in which the HEI is organised has a fundamental impact on staff responsibilities and its overall efficiency
- *Roles* are high-level tasks performed by individuals with identifiable knowledge and skills, supporting business processes
- *Workgroups* are groups of people with differing roles and, perhaps from different departments, working together, either informally or formally to achieve shared goals. The organisational structure will not necessarily reflect workgroups.

People

It is necessary to keep in mind all the external relationships which exist between the HEI and other organisations. A picture is useful to show which bodies have control over it and which are controlled by it, and any other links.

Figure 7.1 shows an HEI with examples of users, service providers, influencers and related agencies. When describing your own architecture it is important to identify these groups for your own HEI and take account of their needs and influence.

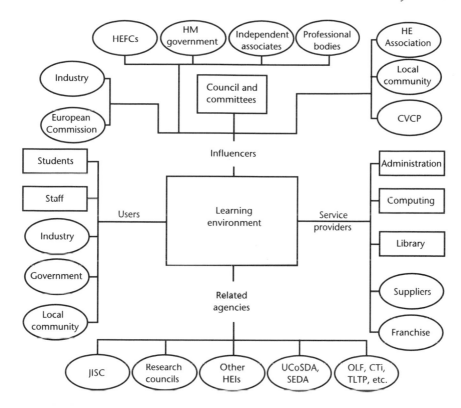

Figure 7.1 A learning environment with external relationships

In Figure 7.1 the HEI itself is shown in rectangular boxes and the external units in ellipses. The types and flows of information between them should be captured by a process model.

The business processes defined in the previous chapter are operated by staff, subcontractors and possibly franchisees. If there are mismatches between business systems and objectives, people can usually compensate for them, but at the expense of their own job efficiency. This has the effect that if future organisational changes are not supported by appropriate business systems, people may not be so accommodating.

The roles that people perform are described later in this chapter. Details such as skills, culture, career structures and so on can be included, though they are outside the scope of this book.

Organisational structure

Organisational structures should facilitate the institution's attainment of its business objectives; structures should serve the key business processes. In too many cases the structures determine the processes, making some (valuable) processes difficult or impossible and generating structure-maintaining processes which are at best incidental to the main objectives of the organisation.

Review of organisational structure is an important element in developing and managing a learning environment. The Jarratt Report (CVCP 1985) caused most of the chartered universities to review their organisational structures, bringing, in many cases, a streamlining of operation, a better integration of academic, financial and physical planning, and clearer lines of accountability. Similarly, the Education Reform Act of 1988 prescribed certain forms of organisational structure for the new institutions; the Further Education Act of 1992 significantly increased the number able to use 'university' in their titles. Most HEIs, then, have paid recent attention to their internal organisation and have accepted the spirit of recommendations concerning efficient and accountable decision making. This means that most are open to modest organisational changes which might be needed to improve the learning environment, but are unlikely (or unable) to take on board radical organisational change.

In reviewing the need for change, consequent upon a recognition of the need to manage and develop the learning environment, an HEI will have to identify ways in which its existing structure currently serves, and inhibits, the processes needed for efficient and effective management and development of the learning environment. It will also have to investigate ways in which such processes, and indeed the processes of learning, teaching and innovation in teaching, are actually supported by informal or unofficial organisational structures. The role of informal structures – e.g. support networks of enthusiasts for new teaching methods – should not be underestimated. In many ways, they are prototypical of the more fluid forms of organisation valued by evangelists for new methods of business organisation. For the HEI, the key organisational task is to see that individuals and informal or ad hoc organisations play a productive part in shaping the learning environment.

Formal organisational structures

HEIs differ widely in the details of their internal organisation. There are significant differences between:

- Oxford and Cambridge
- The chartered college-based universities (e.g. Durham, Lancaster)
- The (larger number of) chartered universities which do not have colleges
- The new universities (many of them formerly polytechnics) which became higher education corporations under the 1988 Education Reform Act.

There are also significant differences between English and Scottish institutions and among the Scottish institutions.

Most HEIs have an organisational structure in which there are two important decision-making bodies. The names vary, but one of these (often called a senate or academic board) has responsibility for the great majority of the academic affairs of the HEI. The other (often called a council or a board of governors) has responsibility for resources, particularly for finance and staffing. In some HEIs, these bodies are treated with some equality. In many, senate is constrained by council. In most of the 'new' universities, the board of governors has clear authority over the academic board. In most HEIs the council has a majority of lay members. In higher education corporations, this majority (of 'independent members' of the board of governors) is guaranteed by the provisions of the Education Reform Act. The academic decision making of the staff (and student) bodies is thereby constrained by the resourcing and other decisions of a body in which lay members are the majority.

Council and senate, or their equivalents, cannot transact all the business of the HEI and so they normally discharge some of their functions through other committees. Of these, the most important will be an academic planning board or policy and resources committee, within which academic, financial and physical planning are integrated. (This committee may be a joint committee of senate and council.) The top half of Figure 7.2 shows an example, (let's call it the 'University of Old Windsor' to avoid any attempts to compare it with a real institution) of the structure of the main committees of a chartered English university.

In this case, the Academic Planning Board is a committee of the Senate, but advises Council; there are some joint committees of Senate and Council and Council has clear responsibility for staffing and financial management.

The bottom half of Figure 7.2 shows how the staff of the 'University of Old Windsor' are divided into faculties and into departments within faculties.

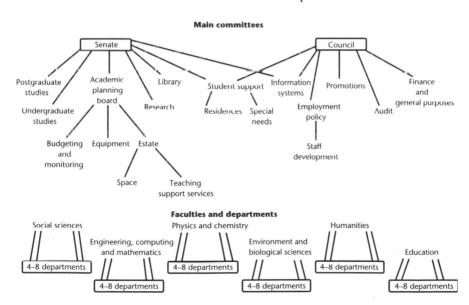

Figure 7.2 Committees, faculties and departments

Each faculty has a faculty board (consisting of all members of the faculty) at which policy issues may be discussed and new course proposals reviewed. Each faculty has a small number of specialist committees (e.g. undergraduate, post-graduate, research, IT, promotions). The faculty also has a Policy and Resources Committee (PRC), consisting of the heads of departments and chaired by the faculty dean. The committee structure is also repeated, with variations, at departmental level.

The links between the organisational structures in the bottom and top halves of Figure 7.2 are of two kinds. First, items of business flow between cognate committees. For example, the university's Equipment Committee annually allocates equipment funds to each of the faculties. Each faculty PRC will deter-mine the allocation of equipment funds between departments. Course pro-posals flow in the opposite direction: beginning with discussion in the appropriate committee at departmental level and moving upwards through a process of approval which (in this institution) involves discussion by *six* com-mittees before reaching Senate. Second, many of the university committees (top half of the diagram) largely consist of representatives of the faculties. The Academic Planning Board, for example, includes all the deans of faculties.

Figures 7.3a and b introduce the final, and probably the most important, element in understanding the organisational structure. Although the formal powers of the institution are deeply interwoven in its committee structure, much of the business of the institution is strongly shaped and executed by senior academics and directors of services. The relationship between these individuals' powers and action (on the one hand) and the formal committee structure (on the other hand) is rarely simple. In some HEIs, notably those organised as higher education corporations, considerably greater power may be vested in individuals and small executive, or management, groups – notably the vice-chancellor or his/her equivalent, and other members of the directorate.

Formal organisational structure and management of the learning environment

In the example HEI represented in the committees, faculties and depart-ments in Figure 7.2, the kinds of decisions needed to develop and manage the forms of learning environment we are describing in this book are dis-tributed across a number of loosely connected or unconnected committees. The process of course approval involves six committees, but there is no formal involvement of committees which manage the library or information systems services. Departmental staff-student committees frequently complain about the quality of simple teaching resources (OHPs, furniture) in the university's shared teaching spaces but there are no direct links to the Teaching Support Services committee (itself a backwater of Estates). Innovation in teaching methods is promoted by an independent unit which has no direct links to academic planning processes at any level.

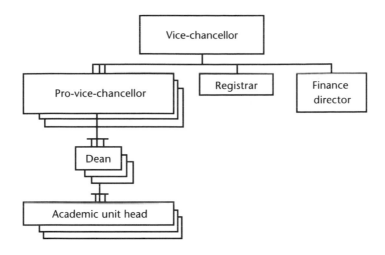

Figure 7.3a Typical traditional line management structure

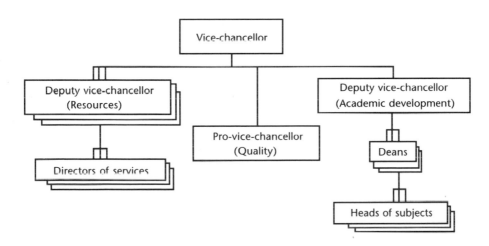

Figure 7.3b New university structure

However, the pattern of involvement of senior academics and directors of services in these various committees enables information flow and *some* coordination despite discontinuities in the committee structure. In addition, informal or ad hoc task groups help to coordinate and promote information flow, even though they may lack formal powers or control over resources. (In the example HEI, an informal Learning Technology Advisory Group with members from Information Systems Services, Staff Development, the Innovation in Higher Education Unit carries out some of this work.)

As we argued in Chapter 6, effective management of the learning environment, especially in times of resource scarcity, demands a high degree of integration between the processes which provide the (subject-independent) learning infrastructure and the department-level processes which provide subject-specific learning opportunities for the student. In addition, the kinds of transformation enabled and necessitated by new technology require a strategic commitment at high level within the institution, a capacity to make strategic choices which are well informed about new educational and technological opportunities, and the ability to see that this commitment permeates all levels and areas of the institution's organisational structure.

The question each HEI will have to ask is whether its current organisational structures are capable of meeting these needs. If they are not, what changes to the formal or informal structures will be required, which are possible, and which are urgent?

Roles

In previous chapters we described the business processes and how the business trends affect the way in which HEIs, and therefore the employees and contractors, operate.

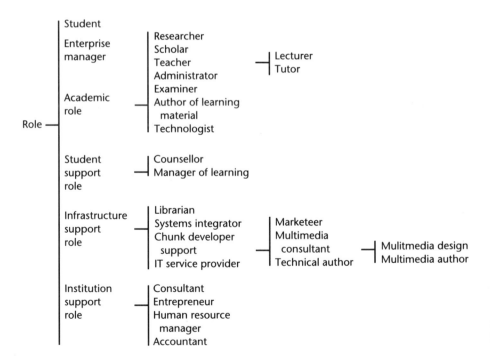

Figure 7.4 Types of role

Business processes are broken down into tasks carried out by employees. An individual employee carrying out a specific task is performing a role.

It is essential to check that roles map exactly to the business processes or inefficiencies will occur. By capturing the different roles it is possible to check for mismatches of resources and correct this by retraining and redeploying staff where necessary. Figure 7.4 is an example of a role type hierarchy tree. It will be useful for you to complete one of these using your own HEI's roles.

An individual can be responsible for carrying out more than one role and several people can be responsible for carrying out the same role. There may be IT support for the role; and as the degree of IT support increases, the role of the employee will be changed. The individual carries out the role in a work-place which is defined in the next chapter.

Employees and those people interfacing with a learning environment can be classified broadly into the following groups:

- Academic staff
- Students
- Academic support staff
- Institution support staff.

Some roles may be outsourced. As an example, the next section looks in some detail at the roles that will be carried out by the academic staff group. It will be important for an institution to do this expansion for all the other staff groups that it identifies as populating its learning environment.

Academic staff roles

Examples of academic staff roles, and some of the pressures and issues relating to them, are as follows:

- *Researcher/scholar* – this is an extremely important role for most academic staff, many of whom gain a great deal of their job satisfaction from it. Most academic staff are also under great pressure to engage in various forms of research and scholarship for more instrumental reasons. These include promotion, winning external funding for the department, and contributing to the department's profile in the research assessment exercise. The rewards associated with success in research can be seen as a disincentive to innovation in teaching
- *Teacher (lecturer/tutor)* – while this is the role that occupies most time for the majority of academic staff, it is often regarded as the poor cousin to research. There remains a strong resistance in higher education to the recognition and rewarding of teaching excellence, and this can be a brake on teaching innovation. Unpacking the role of 'teacher', with the consequent focus on learning, could redress this. Traditionally the teacher carries out a repetitive and undemanding role – that of lecturing to a passive audience. Fostering student learning, on the other hand, requires greater professionalism and flexibility, for example in designing learning

tasks, selecting and adapting resources, using a wide range of assessment methods and giving individualised feedback

- *Administrator* – just as, in some ways, teaching is traditionally viewed as an amateur activity requiring no special training so, too, is administration. In the older universities, many administrative duties are rotated around teaching staff, regardless of their interest or expertise. This is hard to sustain, as pressures from all quarters add to the burden of heads of departments and other cost centre managers. As the system expands, there is increasing recognition of the need for professionalism in academic administration, opening up new opportunities for specialisation in this role
- *Counsellor* – with the rapid expansion of numbers in higher education in the 1990s, students are entering the system who would have previously gone elsewhere. This, together with larger class sizes, has invariably led to an increase in the number of students facing difficulties in their studies, so enhancing the need for pastoral care and for counsellors who can provide it. It also enhances the need for academic and learning support staff to be capable of 'front line' support and sensitive referral
- *Manager of learning* – with the move to modularisation, students are ceasing to be the responsibility of a single academic department. They need advice on the selection of modules if they are to create a coherent course of study. Academic staff who are to meet this need should have knowledge of or, at least, access to information on, all modules taught by their institution
- *Assessor* – HEIs are regarded as custodians of academic standards. Academic staff are sometimes squeezed between this and the need to produce students with good grades. Hence a pressure on the teacher as formal assessor or 'examiner'. The other assessment role is giving students formative feedback on their progress. The rapid expansion of the system has challenged HEIs to find new ways of performing this role, which is vital to student learning
- *Author of learning material* – traditionally the creation of learning material – whether in the form of handouts, lecture notes or textbooks – is an individual endeavour. A departmental, team, approach to the task, involving colleagues from learning support sections, is rare. This is increasingly a problem, as the development and use of more sophisticated media requires economy of effort and specialisation in roles, normally provided only by a team approach. To justify the investment in high quality learning material also means that such materials are subsequently used by more than one or two members of staff. As the MacFarlane Report (1992: 2) put it:

> The question of the most efficient, effective or appropriate teaching methods will no longer be a matter for decision by a single teacher. There is now a pressing need to increase efficiency and provide economies in the processes of teaching and learning. At present, institutions pay an unacceptably high price for courses that are independently designed, produced and delivered.

- *Technologist* – practically all academic staff have come to terms with IT as part of their working lives, for example, using a word processor. As IT is increasingly used to support student learning in a variety of ways, the academics' capability in, and awareness of, the use of IT has to increase, especially as their students often demonstrate more competence than their teachers
- *Consultant* – HEIs encourage staff to act as consultants as a means of enhancing the institution's reputation, developing a distinctive strand of action research
- *Entrepreneur* – academic staff have become accustomed to seeking funds from a variety of sources. Additionally, they are being increasingly called on to sell their HEI to prospective students. For example, recruitment fairs and visits to colleges in the Far East have become a regular part of academic life.

These examples of the roles of academic staff highlight the importance of clearly defining the role to the business need. In the changing world of HEIs it could be argued that the future roles of academic staff will be less as pure presenters of knowledge and more as authors and developers of learning material and managers of learning. To achieve this successfully they will need to reassess their attitude to the question of reuse of learning materials, by themselves and others, and the institution will need to provide more professional support staff to support the delivery of the essential functions. Additionally, systematic staff development needs to be provided for academic staff, particularly in the area of integration of IT into the learning processes. The variety of academic roles essential for the creation of a successful learning environment needs to recognised and appropriately rewarded. Institutions need to address the issue of specialisation; given the variety of roles and the different skill sets needed for each, what role should each individual academic play? This suggests a much more proactive human resources strategy than is common at present, with, for example, more specific job descriptions, frequent appraisal, focused development opportunities and new career pathways.

Workgroups

Workgroups are groups of people with differing roles, and possibly from different departments working together, either informally or formally, to achieve shared goals. The organisational structure will not necessarily reflect workgroups. They may be permanent, in which case they may well be defined as part of the organisational structure, or they may be temporary, set up to complete a particular project and disbanded on its completion.

Several models are available. Diana Laurillard (1993), for example, has proposed that wider use be made of the kinds of course team arrangement evolved by the Open University. With the increase in modularisation and

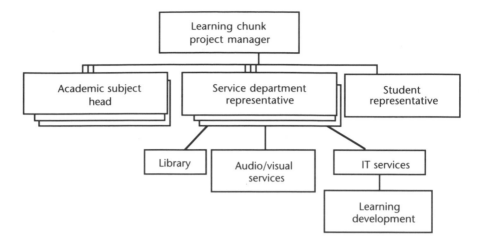

Figure 7.5 Learning chunk development team

cross-disciplinary teaching, matrix forms of organisation become more attractive. Figure 7.5 is an example.

Resources, particularly staff time, are controlled by heads of departments and deans of faculty (in the case of academic staff) and by heads of services (in the case of support staff). A course team – or, in our conception, the set of people responsible for creating and managing a learning chunk – could reasonably include academic staff drawn from one or more departments, learning technology specialists (e.g. those with skills in constructing computer-based learning resources), and representatives of the services which provide the learning environment infrastructure.

Matrix organisation is one way of facilitating better integration at the operational level but it is not in itself a solution to the larger problem of ensuring that the organisation can respond rapidly to change, make strategic commitments which are well informed about educational and technological opportunities, and monitor the alignment between key objectives, processes and structures. This requires an appropriate balance between delegating to the academic departments the ability to chase new opportunities as they see them (rewarding them for success in this task), and ensuring the coherence between the evolving activity of academic departments and the overall mission, organisation, infrastructure and resources of the institution. The increasing delegation of budgets and setting up of cost/profit centres at departmental level is a trend moving in the right direction.

If we consider the learning process model, repeated for clarity as Figure 7.6, we can exemplify how workgroups might be implemented. For example, the chunk development process will probably involve these roles, among others:

- The academic as author of learning materials
- The librarian as information provider
- CAL developer
- Graphics designer
- Programmer
- Project manager.

When a new learning chunk has been accepted for development it may well be established as a project, and a team or workgroup containing the above roles established to carry out the development work. The team members would come from different departments in the organisation structure but would accept the common goal. This team would probably be disbanded on successful implementation of the learning chunk. It is likely that a separate workgroup would be set up for each new learning chunk. The roles would be the same and in some cases the people would be the same, but this project framework implies a temporary group.

However, if we consider the institution management, department management and learning environment management processes it is likely that each of these key processes will be controlled by some form of committee, with, almost certainly, a significant overlap of individuals within them. We recommend that these processes are of a continuous iterative nature, and so we would see these committees as examples of permanent workgroups.

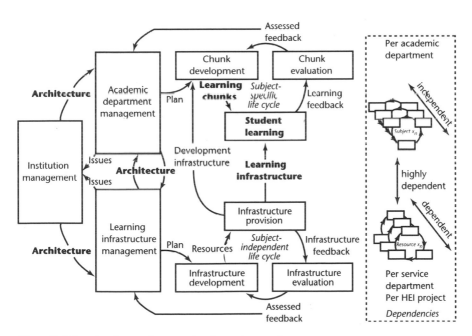

Figure 7.6 Developing and managing learning environments

In Chapter 3, where we discussed the management of change, we identified the need to establish a vision for an institution. This vision will be an element of the architecture under the responsibility of the workgroup controlling the institution management process. We also raised the need to establish a strategy planning team to determine the institution's business strategy. This will also be an element of the architecture and this team (or workgroup) will need to be an integral part of the structure responsible for these processes.

In more traditional terms, these workgroups may well equate to such groups as the senate, the academic planning committee and the information services committee, among others. They will need to involve the vice-chancellor, pro-vice-chancellors, deans, heads of academic departments, service department heads, for example the librarian and director of IT, and others.

Each institution will need to review its current organisation to ensure that it establishes the right workgroups, involving the right people, and correct lines of communication between them, if they are to ensure that their key management processes are effectively implemented.

What next?

This chapter has described the elements of the social system. You now need to capture for your HEI a picture of the external groups and bodies with which the HEI interfaces, the organisational structure (both current and targeted if these are different), the roles people perform, and which workgroups are required. You must ensure that roles and workgroups are aligned to the business processes and the business needs.

Just as HEIs need to take focused decisions on their use of IT, so too they need to deploy their human resources strategically. This involves negotiating and agreeing the roles and responsibilities of different groups of staff, particularly academic and learning support staff. The process is likely to lead to changes from the current position. Staff in learning support centres, for example, are likely to take on increased responsibility for supporting student learning, and academics to specialise in one or more of the roles outlined in this chapter. Academic and learning support staff are likely to develop team skills as they jointly build the learning environment infrastructure, for example through the development and adaptation of materials and software for student learning.

The social system is used as input to the definition of workplaces in Chapter 8 and the technical system in Chapter 9.

8

Workplaces and Services

This chapter defines the major work-places used by an institution's staff and students. It discusses the services required at these workplaces and the different ways in which these services may be provided.

The trends towards open and distance learning signal important changes in a student's workplaces. You should use this chapter to help formulate your response to these changes.

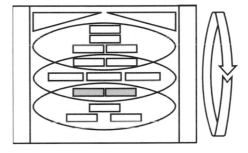

A workplace is a person's working environment. It includes any technical components needed to deliver the services required by the role or roles they perform there. The workplace forms the bridge between the roles performing business processes and the technical systems providing services to support them. The allocation of roles to workplace is best described by the workplace model (Figure 8.1).

Workplace model

The workplace model identifies the different workplaces used in an institution, groups them into like types and shows which roles use which workplaces.

The model classifies the workplaces at the top level into on-campus, off-campus and other miscellaneous workplaces. On-campus refers to both the institution's own campus or campuses and those of other institutions.

Under on-campus workplace you will find resource centre, lecture theatre and campus room. These are all types of on-campus workplace. Under resource centre you will find video conference studio, laboratory, HEI video-on-demand facility and the HEI library. These are all types of resource centre workplace. By classifying workplaces into a type hierarchy like this you will create a tree with more general workplaces near to the root (the left) and more specific, specialised workplaces towards the leaves (the right).

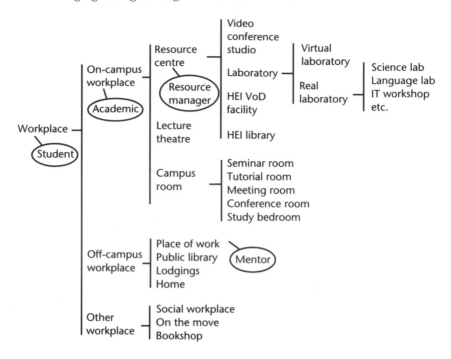

Figure 8.1 The learning environment workplace model

Associated with resource centre you will find a resource manager. This association illustrates that the role resource manager works at a resource centre. Since laboratory, HEI library, and so on are all resource centres it is implied that each may have a resource manager. In this case as the workplaces become more specialised so does the role of the resource manager. The increasing specialisation of the role and of the workplace at which the role is carried out will call for specialised services to be provided, over and above those common services provided to all resource managers.

Associated with the root workplace you will find the student role. This illustrates that a student works at all the workplaces. In this case the services required by the student role are not different at the different workplaces. The challenge here is to find alternative ways of providing the same services to the various workplaces.

The remainder of this chapter concentrates on the needs of the student role.

In order to ensure that your learning environment provides the right services at the right workplaces for your staff, trading partners and students, you should complete this workplace model. Add in further workplaces as required and ensure that all the roles identified in your social system have at least one workplace.

Services and service provision

A step-by-step approach to identifying the services required by a learning environment is given below, first at a general level and later, more specifically, at a level related to the needs of the student learning process.

Identifying learning environment services

First, identify service requirements by analysis of the operations on business objects:

- Select a business object, for example a learning chunk, from the learning environment (Figure 8.2)
- List operations required for the object, for example establish market need, specify, create, develop, maintain, promote, provide, evaluate, improve, withdraw
- Each of these is a high-level service: learning chunk market research, learning chunk specification, learning chunk creation, etc.
- For each high-level service develop a process model identifying lower-level processes, business objects and allocating roles to these processes

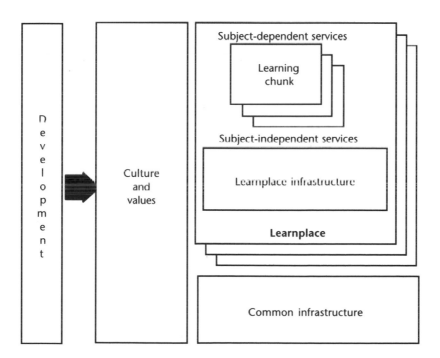

Figure 8.2 The learning environment model

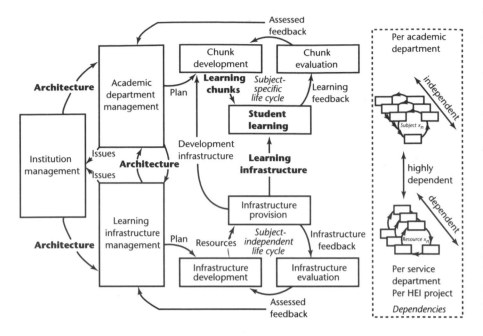

Figure 8.3 Developing and managing learning environments

- Identify lower-level services by analysis of the role as in the following step 2.

Second, identify service requirements by analysis of a role's needs implied by the processes they perform:

- Select a business process, for example chunk evaluation, from the learning environment (Figure 8.3)
- Decompose the process identifying lower-level processes such as assess student, aggregate student performance, measure industry relevance
- Allocate roles to subprocesses, for example for assess student, tutor defines tests, student performs tests
- Identify services to support the role, for example for tutor defined tests, access to learning chunk details, access to other tests, test development guidance.

Identifying services supporting student learning

Analysis of the student learning process in Chapter 6 led us to a number of mandatory learning functions for a learning environment and a variety of learning methods currently employed to provide these functions. Using the general approach described above, we can identify a number of high-level services required by a student role involved in the student learning process.

A student will require, for example, lecturing services, tutoring services and mentoring services.

A finer-grained view of these services may be established by following a step-by-step approach.

First, select a learning method from your learning method table. Remember you can extend the list of learning methods and learning functions as appropriate to your institution. The example below uses the table of learning methods and learning functions given in Table 6.1.

Learning methods	Orientation	Motivation	Presentation	Clarification	Elaboration	Confirmation
Tutorial	Medium	Medium	Low	High	High	Medium

Second, map to the learning functions. In the above example the table shows that the tutorial learning method provides high coverage for feedback, clarifying and elaborating.

Third, using Table C.2 in Appendix C, Twelve subprocesses of student learning, access the appropriate learning-initiated cells.

Learning function	Description	Tutor initiated	Learner initiated
Feedback	For example, as a consequence of hypothesis making – Am I on the right track?	Provide instructionally relevant, timely feedback	Seek answers to self-posed questions

These cells define tasks for the student. Services supporting these tasks will complement the learning method. In the example here one task is 'seek answers to self-posed questions'. A service which helps students answer self-posed questions would, therefore, complement the tutorial learning method.

We recommend that you extend the tables in Appendix C to build yourself a tool for innovation in the construction of learning tasks and services to support them.

Selecting alternative ways to provide the services

Once you have identified the services required you can consider alternative ways of providing these services. The examples given in this book are based on an analysis considering the high-level services identified above. Mechanisms for service provision are classified in Figure 8.4.

The changing student profile recognises the students' need for more freedom in their choice of time and location for learning. Table 8.1 positions

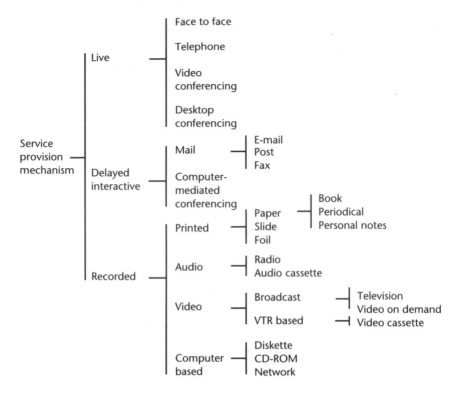

Figure 8.4 Mechanisms for service provision

the service provision mechanisms according to their time and location characteristics and provides a few examples to start you off. You should use it to help choose which mechanisms to provide for each service you identify. When you are completing your own table do not forget the dimension of pace, which is also important. You may find it useful to prepare tables for pace against time and pace against place.

Table 8.1 Service provision characterised by time and place

	Fixed location	*Restricted location*	*Open location*
Fixed time	Face-to-face lecture	Video conference	TV broadcast
Restricted time	Face-to-face mentoring	Work placement	
Open time	Paper-based reference material	Video on demand	Paper-based material

Table 8.2 Learnplace table

Learnplace name	Learning method	Student workplace	Provision mechanism
Live lecture	Lecture	Lecture theatre	Face to face
VTR lecture	Lecture	Accommodation	Video cassette
Home VoD lecture	Lecture	Accommodation	Video on demand
HEI VoD lecture	Lecture	HEI VoD facility	Video on demand
TV lecture	Lecture	Accommodation	TV broadcast
Video conference lecture	Lecture	Video conference studio	Face to face
Telephone conference lecture	Lecture	Accommodation	Telephone conference
Live tutorial	Tutorial	Campus room	Face to face
Video conference tutorial	Tutorial	Video conference studio	Video conference
Home tutorial	Tutorial	Accommodation	Computer mediated
Home tutorial	Tutorial	Accommodation	Desktop conference
Live practical	Practical	Laboratory	Face to face
Work placement	Practical	Place of work	Face to face
Virtual practical	Practical	Virtual laboratory	Computer based
Home practical	Practical	Accommodation	Computer based
Public practical	Practical	Public facility	Computer based

Learnplaces

A learnplace is a student workplace equipped to support a particular learning method. This concept was introduced in Chapter 5 as a key part of the learning environment. Each HEI should list the learnplaces they plan to support. We identify a learnplace by naming its student workplace, its learning method and how it is equipped to provide services (also known as the service provision mechanism). Some examples of learnplaces are shown in Table 8.2. This is obviously a partial list since we cannot consider all possibilities. You should add your own learning methods, your own provision mechanisms and your own student workplaces. Some examples to consider include mail, computer-mediated conferencing, computer network, diskette and CD-ROM.

Identifying learnplaces

A learnplace is a student workplace equipped to support a particular learning method. A learnplace consists of the following three things:

- A student workplace (from the workplace model)
- A learning method (from the list of methods in Table 6.1)
- A service provision mechanism (from the service provision model).

A potential learnplace is therefore identified by taking a student workplace and a learning method and considering how the services required by the method may be provided at this workplace.

In our examples we have identified eight methods, about 20 workplaces and about 20 provision mechanisms; you may well identify more of each which you consider to be appropriate. While not all combinations are sensible, this gives us (8×20×20) 3200 potential learnplaces to consider!

Aggregation to contain complexity

In order to reduce the complexity of all these possible learnplaces without missing key elements in the learning environment, we suggest that you use the higher-level workplaces and higher-level provision mechanisms. The higher-level workplaces and provision mechanisms are located towards the left of the models, or nearer the root.

Aggregated learnplaces contain more than one workplace or service provision mechanism. Elemental learnplaces contain only one workplace and one service provision. You can group elemental learnplaces together to provide a single aggregated learnplace, and so contain the complexity of the learnplaces.

Higher-level provision mechanism example

If we consider 'individual study in the library' as an example, 'individual study' is the learning method and 'in the library' is the student workplace. The possible service provision mechanisms are all concerned with providing the student with access to recorded material. Rather than listing all low-level provision mechanism possibilities we could use the higher-level service provision mechanisms. For example instead of:

• Individual study in the library with physical access to books
• Individual study in the library with physical access to periodicals
• Individual study in the library with access to other types of recorded material,

we could use the higher-level provision mechanism:

• Individual study in the library with physical access to printed material
• Individual study in the library with physical access to audio cassette
• Individual study in the library with physical access to other recorded materials.

This will decrease the actual number of learnplaces we need to list, but the mechanism will exist for further expansion when necessary.

We can go even higher in the service provision mechanism tree and produce the following learnplace:

• Individual study in the library with physical access to recorded material.

On the service provision mechanism tree this would also include TV broadcast, video on demand and radio. For study in the library these would not be appropriate and so you might want to exclude them. Now we have:

- Individual study in the library with physical access to recorded material excluding TV broadcast, VoD and radio.

Here we have a definition of an aggregated learnplace which supports many alternative service provision mechanisms.

Higher-level workplace example
Another way of defining a potential learnplace is to take a learning method and a service provision mechanism and identify all the student workplaces.

For example if we consider 'peer learning', the services required here support peer-to-peer communication. Considering the different workplaces we could identify learnplaces like:

- Peer learning with face-to-face communication in study bedroom
- Peer learning with face-to-face communication in meeting room
- Peer learning with face-to-face communication in another workplace.

In this case we can cover all workplace possibilities by using the top-level workplace, which is student workplace:

- Peer learning with face-to-face communication in student workplace.

Here we have a definition of a single aggregated learnplace which supports many alternative workplaces.

Choosing the right level of aggregation
We can contain complexity by reducing the number of different learnplaces using the aggregation techniques explained above. However, careful judgement is required to ensure that learnplaces requiring different resources to provide the services are separated. An example here might be peer learning using E-mail. In this case a separation of workplace between on-campus and off-campus would be useful to help distinguish between the two service provision mechanisms of remote access E-mail and local access E-mail: peer learning on-campus with local access E-mail, and peer learning off-campus with remote access E-mail.

We have separated these two learnplaces so that their different resource requirements may more easily be discussed. In the first case, access to the campus LAN will be required, while in the second, dial-up access will be required. We could also identify 'peer learning at place of work using E-mail' because in this case the place of work is responsible for service provision.

Learnplace qualities

The different learnplaces you have identified have different characteristics. These can be inherited from:

- *The workplace* – for example the library may be conducive to individual study because it is quiet, free from disturbance

- *The provision mechanism* – for example a video cassette provides no facilities for interaction but is repeatable at the student's discretion
- *The learning method* – for example a lecture is primarily a presentation of material with little opportunity for interaction
- *A combination of workplace, provision mechanism and learning method* – for example a live seminar provides the opportunity for interaction with the leader and also with peers attending the lecture.

In order to understand better the characteristics of your learnplaces you can define them using the OPEN*framework* qualities which were introduced in Chapter 4.

In the example below we show how the qualities can be used to describe the characteristics of the student using a computer-aided learning package. The learning method employed here will depend on the package but, in general, most closely matches presentation with some practical aspects. The workplace will include all student workplaces: at home, on campus, on the train, etc.

Availability

Choice of subject	A large and growing number of packages are available
Choice of location	If a large display is required then restricted to places giving access to desktop workstation otherwise only need access to portable workstation
Choice of time	Unrestricted assuming online access not required
Choice of learning style	Limited, predetermined interaction and elaboration. Non-personal
Access for non-English-speaking student groups	None yet
Access for disabled students	No tailored packages

Usability

The environment motivates the student	Depends on the student's individual learning styles
The environment is congenial and attractive	Unrestricted student choice
Opportunities to apply understanding	Depends on the subject: applies to word processing and other subjects amenable to virtual reality emulations, but not all
Opportunities to review understanding	Some limited predetermined elaboration, possible expansion of sophistication using AI/knowledge-based tools

Performance

Increased employability	No direct relationship currently
Student results	Satisfactory completion of specified packages could be a part of an assessment method
Assessment feedback	Packages will increasingly include more sophisticated feedback machanisms
Adequate learning resources	Packages facilitate focused, small-scope learning and so have the ability to provide good supporting learning material

Security

Pastoral tutoring	Packages may be used to support this need: advice on finance, housing, etc.
Fair pricing for educational services	Packages paid for only if used
Comfortable and enjoyable environment	Unrestricted student choice, subject to availability of workstations/portables
Integrity of assessment/marks	Dependent on package and how assessment feedback is used
Finding employment	Packages may be used to support this need

Potential for change

Flexible learning	Students are free to use or ignore CAL packages. The ability to change or tailor packages is, in general, very restricted
Mobility of learning	Packages are physically mobile. The reputation of a package may vary between institutions
Student-centred learning	The granularity of a CAL package is generally large, and the ability of students or chunk developers to pick and mix parts of packages to construct others is rare
Continuous guidance	Packages can provide limited predetermined guidance. Current delivery mechanisms require full version updates to all students when changes occur

What next?

This chapter has explained the concept of workplaces and how services are delivered to the user there. It provided a detailed description of the workplaces and services for the student.

You now need to write down for each role identified in your social system the workplaces and services required. Then, using the OPENframework qualities, define the workplace requirements. You can use the detailed example provided for the student role to help you do this. This will result in a more complete workplace model. It is likely that you will also extend the service provision mechanisms model.

You also need to build a learnplace table for your institution. How you do this was described in identifying and aggregating learnplaces in this chapter.

You have now identified a detailed set of service requirements for your institution's learning environment. These are grouped together into components in the application layer of the technical architecture presented in the next chapter.

9

Technical System

This chapter defines the technical system. It identifies the key IT components supporting the learning environment. These components are positioned in a layered architecture where components in lower layers provide services to those in higher layers but not vice versa.

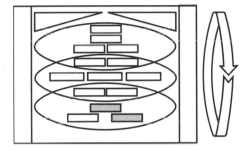

The technical system is described by identifying components which provide the services required by the learning environment. A component is a logical

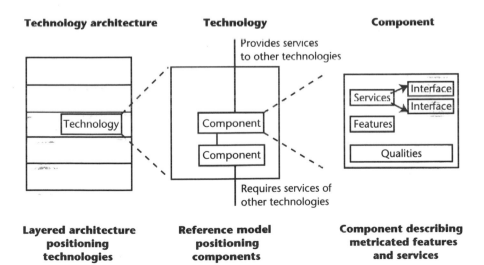

Technology architecture	Technology	Component
Layered architecture positioning technologies	Reference model positioning components	Component describing metricated features and services

Figure 9.1 Technical system components

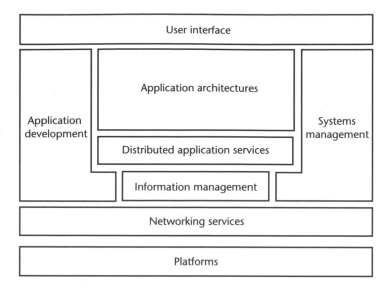

Figure 9.2 The major areas of information technology

part of an IT system and not a product. For example, we might identify the need for a word processor but the choice of vendor and platform (for example, Microsoft Word for Windows) is an implementation option. Specifying the technical system in this way increases potential for change and the longevity of the technical design.

A component identified by analysis of the learning environment processes as described in this book will, in general, be an application component. Such components provide services to a user role through a user interface. In order to provide these services specific to learning environments, they themselves require services provided by more generic components. This approach is summarised in Figure 9.1. The technical system is modelled by dividing it into eight major areas of technology. Each technology area is composed of a number of IT components which provide services to other components and to the user.

The technologies are arranged in layers as shown in the Figure 9.2. These eight areas are discussed in separate sections below:

User interface

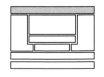

The user interface element covers all aspects of the user interface. It includes the look and feel of the interface style, the enablers used to deliver an application user interface, and the tools used by application developers to develop that interface. It also includes the facilities needed to give users easy access to their applications and to automate parts of their work.

The requirements for access to information can be varied and wide ranging. The underlying requirement is to communicate information between people efficiently and effectively. In addition, some automatic processing of this information by applications can be introduced, thus matching and merging the capabilities of computers and people to provide for information to be handled more easily, clearly and faster. Examples of the services that are visible to the user include video conferencing, video mail, distribution and storage of high quality documents, correspondence imaging, support of information structures, presentation systems, interactive education and training packages, electronic catalogues and information kiosks.

Multimedia incorporates a substantial move to natural user interface, with audio-video services and in the handling of speech commands and queries. Consequently, many applications become more usable as multimedia technology is used to present an interface to humans.

Application architectures

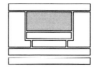

Applications provide the user with the information technology services required by the learning environment. An application architecture identifies the application components, shows their interrelationships and defines the standards to be met by these components. Figure 9.3 identifies the key application components and their relationship.

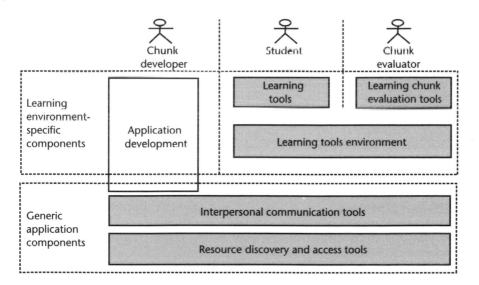

Figure 9.3 Learning environment application architecture

The architecture groups applications according to the type of user role. Three main roles have been considered in Figure 9.3. You should complete the application architecture for your institution by considering the service requirements for all the roles you have identified.

The architecture recognises that the learning environment is composed of applications which are specific to the learning environment, and applications which have more general usage. The learning environment application components are developed by:

• Tailoring generic application components – a gooseberry editor which is an example of a learning chunk development tool could be constructed from a generic word processor which is tailored by the provision of appropriate templates and skeleton files
• Using generic application components – a chunk development coordination application which synchronises the activities of the different geographically and organisationally distributed roles could be constructed from generic workflow and planning tools
• Bespoke learning-environment-specific application development – a fee-payment application which charges for the learning chunk by monitoring learning resource usage is likely to require some bespoke development, although the tailoring of the billing components already in use within the utilities industry may also be possible.

The technical system components supporting the chunk developer are discussed further in the application development section of this chapter. Components supporting the student and the chunk evaluator are discussed here.

Learning tools

There are many types of computer-based learning tools supporting the various learning functions discussed in Chapter 6. Table 9.1 classifies these according to the learning activity they support.

Learning tools environment

The learning tools and the learning chunk evaluation tools will use common components from the learning tools environment to provide integration services. These components will specialise the generic integration services provided by the user interface, information management, distributed application services, networking services and platform technologies to the needs of the learning and chunk evaluation tools. For example, generic information management components will be used to structure, store and retrieve information such that it can be shared between the different tools, and generic messaging components from networking and distributed application services will be used to facilitate the flow of information between the tool types.

Table 9.1 Types of computer-based learning tool

Category	Examples	Comment
Exploring	WWW browsers, multimedia encyclopaedias	These enable students to explore an area of knowledge, following links from one topic to another
Identifying	Search engines, citation indexes	Where students have predetermined questions for which they require answers, effective search engines are required. For effective use students need to be trained in knowledge retrieval and the tools must be sophisticated enough to minimise the number of false 'hits'
Explaining	Tutorial programs	These packages may correspond to lecture courses or to student textbooks. To be easy to incorporate they need to have been designed with modification in mind
Experimenting	Simulations, modelling packages	Using simulation and modelling packages, students can experiment with models of dangerous or expensive equipment and can collapse time to investigate changes that normally take place over months or years
Diagnosing	Student self-tests	Students need regular feedback on their acquisition of knowledge. This can be provided through additions to tutorial packages, or through software
Recording (including note-taking)	Word processing, desktop publishing, drawing packages, laboratory data loggers	Students benefit from applications that facilitate note taking (including use of palmtops) and the presentation of work. Certain subjects will have specialised recording requirements, such as CAD in architecture and engineering
Visualising	Molecular modellers, virtual reality	Applications which enable complex objects, such as molecules, to be represented and manipulated can dramatically assist student understanding. Virtual reality will rapidly find new application areas in education
Learning management (including informing and promoting)	Computer-managed learning, campus information systems, information systems, student record systems	The variety of learning resources available requires systems to inform students of what is available and to advise them on appropriate use. Benefits for HEIs will be maximised if information about resources and student use of resources is integrated
Presentation	Desktop presentation packages	When producing materials to suport paper-based and face-to-face learning activities, communication is assisted by use of appropriate presentation software

Resource discovery and access tools

There are a large number of resource discovery tools and a large number of overlapping resource spaces in use today. These could be classified by access mechanism, which would include Gopher, World Wide Web, ftp sites, directory systems, distributed file systems and so on.

The tools support two methods of locating resources: by browsing and by searching. The browse tools allow the user to navigate a predetermined set of relationships between resources. These include tools to navigate the directories of file systems, tools to traverse the hyperlinks of hypertext systems, and so on.

The search tools allow the user to locate resources by giving values to particular attributes. For example, they can be used to find a resource of type person whose name is P. Goodyear, or an article by P. Ford with CAL in the title. They include tools which search directory systems, database systems, file systems and so on. Currently, searching is restricted by how resources are designated and described. For example, in one system a web page is designated by its URL (Uniform Resource Locator), a person by their Internet address or X.400 address, an article by its title and author; in another, different descriptors will be used. Better mechanisms are needed to effect more consistent identification of resources and to improve the exchange of this identification information between systems.

Interpersonal communication tools

The student learning process described in Chapter 6 exposed the need for elaboration, clarification and confirmation activities in successful learning. These activities require personal communication between the student and staff or the student and their peers or predecessors. Chapter 8 explained how these

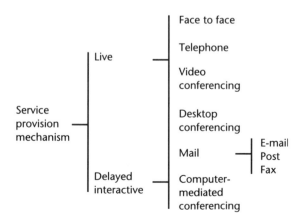

Figure 9.4 Service provision mechanisms for personal communication

requirements could be implemented at various student workplaces through different service provision mechanisms. These are summarised in Figure 9.4.

The tools which provide these services include computer-mediated conferencing systems, E-mail systems, desktop conferencing systems, video conferencing systems and the telephone. Various specialisations of these generic tools are developed to support the student. For example, E-mail systems are configured and tailored to provide student helpline services.

Distributed application services

Distributed application services cover the construction, integration and operation of large-scale systems, composed of separate application systems (or other autonomous application components) linked together.

Currently, distributed application services are primarily concerned with improving the quality of communications between people by the use of information technology. The initial technologies in this area include desktop conferencing, video conferencing and electronic mail carrying multimedia information. IT will support excellent interaction between people who are separated geographically. Communications systems will provide for information to be readily and economically transferred between individuals and, when needed, simultaneous access. The IT equipment will deal with information received from other systems; it will understand how to present it and how to handle its characteristics and relationships without loss of information.

Information management

Information management enables information to be modelled, stored, retrieved and exchanged between information systems. You should use this technology to maximise the value of the institution's investment in information, by safeguarding it, by making it reusable, and by providing it in the forms needed by its users. You should also use this technology to facilitate the effective reuse of information provided from other sources. These sources will include partnership relationships, both business partners and inter-institutional collaborations, UK reuse initiatives, like TLTP and many other sources from around the world.

One strategy to promote reuse is the formalisation of policy, covering frameworks, methods, techniques, information meta-models, templates and formats, together with the acceptance and implementation by all those involved. While this approach does lead to more immediately reusable information fragments, it also reduces the number of sources. This strategy should certainly be adopted by teams working closely together for an institution's department. They should define and adopt detailed policies to maximise reuse of information within the department. Ideally, these department policies would be specialisations of the set of policies adopted by the institution as a whole. This approach maximises reuse between the departments of an institution while also allowing for local enhancment and refinement to support the more department-specific needs. An institution's policies promoting reuse should be based on UK and internationally agreed standards where possible, to improve the ability to reuse information from as many sources as possible. It is important to recognise that information which does not obey the policies may still be reused but at a higher cost.

Application development

The application development element covers the selection, design, implementation, integration and evolution of the applications needed to support an institution's learning environment. This includes applications which are a part of the learning infrastructure and applications which are a part of a learning chunk.

This section concentrates on the technical system components required to support the development of a learning chunk, see page 78. These components provide services to the chunk developer.

The development of learning infrastructure applications is not covered explicitly in this book. For more information on the development of these applications refer to Chapter 9 of the *Local Government Architecture* publication – see Appendix A.

The reference model for learning chunk development is shown in Figure 9.5. The components supporting learning chunk development are shown divided into two groups: those specifically tailored to the development of learning chunks, and more general components concerned with the processing of information and the management of development projects.

Learning chunk development components

These components are specifically tailored to support the chunk developers in their planning, analysing, designing and implementing of learning chunks. This process is described in more detail in Chapter 6, 'Chunk development'. It is recognised that there are often many different people involved in chunk development, which requires a number of specialist skills. Generally, a development team is established comprising a number of people from both within and outside the institution, who undertake the various chunk developer roles.

While there will often be some overlap between the set of tools used by students in their learning and the set of tools used by chunk developers, there are some tools which are specific to chunk developers. It therefore makes sense to think of chunk development tools being used in a separate chunk

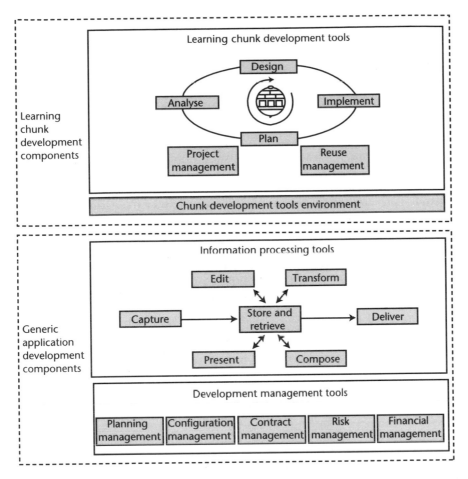

Figure 9.5 Learning chunk development reference model

development environment which is properly tailored to supporting the chunk development process and, in particular, to integrating the parts of a learning chunk.

Learning chunk development components fall into two major types: learning chunk development tools, and chunk development tools environment.

Learning chunk development tools
These tools are used directly by the many different chunk developers. The tools are supported by components from the chunk development tools environment which provides them with integration services. There are a number of different types of tool which are aligned to the development process.

Planning and analysing
There are many generic tools available supporting planning and analysis (see OPEN*framework Application Development*, Appendix A) which may be specialised to the needs of learning chunk development. Further tools are required to support the processes unique to the planning and analysis phases of learning chunk development.

Setting objectives
These processes include the setting and updating of learning objectives which are highly dependent on the quality of their inputs. Tools are needed which help ensure that chunk developers have access to current (though forward-looking), authoritative, well-formed statements about what needs to be learned. Given the two sources of input (see Chapter 6) such tools need to support close ongoing interaction between chunk developers and those working in relevant areas of industry and academic research. The base level tools needed by objective-setters, then, are essentially resource discovery and access tools, though possibly specialised to their needs. There are special tool requirements concerned with facilitating productive forms of interaction within and between academic, professional, industrial and work-based communities.

At a higher level, tools are needed which support the synthesis of information, for example in transforming a multiplicity of statements about vocational needs into a coherent whole. Specialised tools can also help ensure that statements generated by a learning or training needs analysis are appropriately rendered in terms of learning objectives.

At the output end of the instructional objectives-setting process, the tools become less specialised, for example standard text-processing tools.

Defining assessment methods
The process of defining appropriate assessment procedures is tightly coupled with the process of objective-setting. While standards for objective-setting vary, some of the more stringent standards insist that objectives be phrased in language which is geared to testing, for example 'behavioural objectives' which define what is to be learned in terms of observable learner behaviours. It is not appropriate to insist that all worthwhile learning should be measurable in this way. But the definition of assessment procedures should be a principled process, and tools can be used which support a careful mapping between assessment tasks and learning objectives. Such tools are particularly useful when there are complex (e.g. one-to-many) relationships between assessment tasks and learning objectives.

Designing
Aligning learning chunk parts – tools are available which support the design of learning chunks though they are not yet widely used. They help with such problems as creating and reusing instructional strategies, with linking instructional objectives to learning activities (learntasks), with preserving

instructional design rationales, and with evaluating part-finished learning resources. See, for example, Tennyson and Barron (1994) or de Jong and Sarti (1994).

Mapping objectives to credit information – once a student has demonstrated that they have met the learning objectives of a learning chunk, they should be enabled to get externally recognised credit for their achievement. Various systems and methods are in place which help with this process, including the whole apparatus of NVQs etc. Tools are needed which help the learning chunk developer map the objectives of the learning chunk on to externally recognised systems of qualifications and credit accumulation. Quite powerful tools are currently under trial in the European Credit Transfer system (ECTS) which allow very detailed and contextually sensitive representation of competencies etc. See, for example, NECTAR Project (European Commission 1993) for a description of the '*arbre de connaissance*', which provides a formalism and accompanying tools for the representation of competences.

Implementing
Constructing learning resources – most of the tools attracting attention in HE today are generic information-processing tools geared towards the creation of the presentational components of a learning resource. For example, in the development of computer-based learning programs, most authoring tools help with the creation of the screens which students will see and the sounds they will hear.

Reuse management – tools are needed which ensure that opportunities are not missed to repurpose and reuse existing learning resources. The base level tools here are generic resource discovery and access tools suitable for browsing and searching libraries of (multimedia) learning resources.

More specialised tools include finding and reusing 'semi-finished' learning resources (see, for example, de Jong and Sarti 1994), and the real-time location of external (networked) learning resources during a learntask. Tools for the former are used solely by chunk developers, while the latter may also be used by the courseware program with which the student is interacting.

Project management – tools are needed to help prioritise, initiate, allocate, schedule, monitor, coordinate and progress the development activities. Various generic development management tools exist which support planning, risk, financial and contract management activities. These tools are tailored and integrated as necessary to support the project management of the chunk development activity.

Chunk development tools environment – the generic application development components are tailored and integrated to meet the specific needs of the various chunk developers both individually and working as a team. The chunk development tools environment contains components to provide the necessary integration services. Models of the various forms of integration componentry can be found in OPEN*framework Application Development* (see Appendix A). They include: user interface services, process integration services, data repository services, data integration services and message services. While all these services are required to support the chunk developer they are also needed by the chunk evaluator and the student and so are described, more generally, in the other sections of this chapter: user interface, distributed application services and information management. Process integration is, however, especially relevant to the chunk developers and so is discussed below.

Process integration – these components range from simple user agents, which record and then replay a set of inputs which perform a specific user task, to process support systems, which enact a defined process coordinating the use of tools, resources and people.

Such componentry will be used to facilitate the coordination of geographically and organisationally dispersed chunk developers working together on a single project. This will alleviate some of the burden currently placed on the project manager and will help manage the many intertwined dependencies. For example, if a chunk resource list recommends the reading of particular books then this information can be automatically sent to the library to ensure that they are available when the chunk is provided to the students.

Generic application development components

These components are not specifically tailored to support chunk developers but are more generally applicable to all types of development process. Some may be used directly by the chunk developer, for example planning tools and financial management tools. Others will be used or tailored in the construction of learning chunk development tools, for example team-scoped reuse management tools may be built using generic configuration management tools, chunk description editors may be constructed by tailoring word processors to constrain the description's structure, etc.

Generic application development components fall into two major types: information processing tools and development management tools.

Information processing tools
These processing tools support the capture, editing, transforming, composing, presenting, storage, retrieval and delivery of information of various types, including text, image, 2D and 3D graphics, animation, audio, moving image and composites of these. They are primarily used by the chunk developer to construct learning resources. Their application in the earlier development stages and to other parts of the gooseberry is also possible and noted in the sections below.

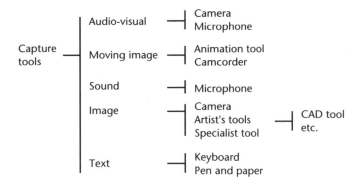

Figure 9.6 Information capture tools

Capture

Traditional information capture components include the keyboard which can provide a text character or a function command, or a mouse which can define a line or the movement of an icon across a screen. These are augmented with components for capturing other information types. Depending upon the type, capture may additionally involve recognising character text from scanned images, scanning image graphics, drawing vector graphics, recording audio sequences, a stills camera providing a bit-mapped frame of a picture, recording video sequences, or various methods of capturing computational data. These tools are shown in Figure 9.6.

Editing

Various editing tools provide browsing facilities and support creation, update, combination and deletion of all information types.

Transforming

Transformation tools translate information between one form or representation and another. Many transformation tools will be used by the chunk developer constructing learning material, for example, converting graphics, compressing images, etc. Transformation tools may additionally be used in earlier development stages and for other parts of the gooseberry, for example syntactic recognition transformation tools such as those which convert voice to text may be used to prepare digests for the marketing section.

Composing and presenting

These tools retrieve information from the storage system and compose it into a form suitable for presentation to human perception. The presentation process involves taking the information and presentation styles and producing a perceptible form of the information which can be presented on output device(s) appropriate to the different types contained in the composite. The direct presentation components include printers, display screens and loudspeakers, with high quality visual or audible presentation. In addition, intermediate forms may be composed that are eventually intended for human perception, such as CD-ROM.

Delivering
These tools provide for information to be transmitted to a recipient. They provide for storage by the recipient within a structured organisation. They provide for search facilities to enable information to be selected using various search criteria. In the case of multimedia, the size of some content portions (e.g. images, audio, motion video) can make it sensible to reference them and to transmit, deliver or store them separately.

Systems management

Systems management enables service providers to manage complex multi-vendor information systems. Systems management tools and enablers help service providers to deliver the required services to users in accordance with service level agreements where relevant. They manage the resources of the information system, ranging from the basic infrastructure (network components, computers, operating systems, databases, filestores, etc.) to the applications providing services to the institution, its students and its partners.

The information systems supporting an institution are being split into many related objects: departments own and run their own systems, students own (or borrow) their own machines, and learning material is made available is many different forms both on and off-campus. Systems management technology and processes must be employed to give the service provider and managers confidence that this growth in complexity can be managed effectively.

The systems management process can be described in ten stages or tasks:

• Operations – involves controlling and monitoring the managed resources in the information system, e.g. how do we ensure that all students are using appropriate versions of software, how do we inform them when changes will affect them, what helpdesk support do we provide, etc.
• Problem – involves diagnosing, fixing and preventing the occurrence of problems, e.g. how do we collect and review evidence of a problem, how do we schedule skills and resources to look at the problem, if we have overseas students do we have to provide 24-hour cover, etc.
• Capacity – involves reviewing operational data to assess the availability and performance of the systems, e.g. maintaining historical records, aggregating the records over time and groups of objects, transforming information to reflect service provided by a particular domain, raising alerts when all is not well, providing information to help forward planning, etc.
• Service level – involves giving a clear statement of what the information system or domain has to provide and supplying service level achievement

information to enable the overall effectiveness of the system to be monitored

- Change – involves providing mechansims for handling changes to the information system, e.g. defining process definitions for the specification, validation and authorisation of change, scheduling their execution, managing the interfaces to other parts of the systems management activity, ensuring that the change process is meeting time, cost and resource constraints, and raising alerts if necessary, etc.
- Inventory – involves maintaining up-to-date records of the total set of applications, hardware and software components and infrastructure that comprise the information system
- Generation – involves providing the means to generate and subsequently change the configuration of the system
- Distribution – involves providing mechanisms to deliver, install and activate components of the information system, e.g. delivering software and configuration data either over the network or by appropriate media, controlling installation of this data within the target system, activating the data for use, maintaining records of data distribution, managing regression of components where changes are found not to work
- Billing – involves reporting to users and to the institution how the information system is performing and providing costs of services to individuals, teams, departments and the institution as a whole
- New requirements – involves responding to requests for modifications to the infrastructure and for the provision of new applications.

The institution should ensure that all these processes are provided and supported where necessary by systems management software components.

Networking services

The networking services elements support the distribution of users, data and applications, by providing interconnection and interworking services over local and wide area networks.

The higher education environment comprises host application services available on a variety of hardware platforms. These services are accessed from user workstations. Networking services provide the means of interconnection and interaction between the workstations and the host systems.

In the context of teaching and learning, typical hosts might include campus-based courseware servers, module catalogues and student assessment data, while the national and international hosts would include specialised research datasets and electronic journal information. The workstations might be sited at a number of different locations including the campus, the home or the workplace.

Network connectivity is well supported by appropriate standards of which the following are most common:

Ethernet
This technology is widely used within HEI campuses, particularly through-out buildings. It operates at speeds of 10 Mbits/sec. over various media, including coaxial, fibre optic and twisted pair copper cabling. Early ether-net users used Thick Net coaxial cables which are bulky and not always easy to install due to their bending radius. Thin Net coaxial cable is often now used as a lower cost and more flexible substitute, although Thin Net cabling segments are limited to 185 metres with a maximum of thirty connections on each segment. Segments are connected by repeaters which regenerate the data as it moves from one segment to another, and they also provide a level of fault protection.

Use of coaxial cable is now somewhat overshadowed by the use of unshielded twisted pair (UTP) wiring. This allows the use of twisted pair copper wiring from the workstation to star points within wiring closets, pro-vided the distance of each cable run is no more than fifty metres. This struc-tured wiring approach is now very popular; it allows much greater flexibility of use of the cabling and operates at speeds of 100 Mbits/sec. ethernet, pro-vided the cables are of sufficiently high quality.

Fibre Distributed Data Interface (FDDI)
This is increasingly used as a backbone network to interconnect campus buildings. It operates at speeds of 100 Mbits/sec. and consists of two counter-rotating fibre optic rings. This allows data from a station on the FDDI network to be sent to both its left and right neighbours. Should either ring fail, the ring can be looped back by the stations closest to the fault, thereby providing operational resilience until the fault can be corrected. It is now possible to obtain FDDI interfaces for both workstations and hosts; costs of these are expected to fall from the current rather expensive levels.

Integrated Services Digital Network (ISDN)
ISDN is an emerging international standard which covers voice, data and image services. It provides end-to-end simultaneous handling of digitised voice and data traffic, over the public switched telephone network. ISDN offers a means of providing digital connection from the home to a campus network at channel speeds of up to 64 Kbits/sec. It thus has possibilities for up- and downloading student learning materials from the HEI to the home at acceptable (but not high) speeds. At present the tariff structure makes the use of ISDN unattractive for this purpose but tariffs are expected to change.

Metropolitan Area Network (MAN)
A MAN is a pervasive network within a limited geographical area (for example a major city). The provision of local cabling services by local cable companies offers the prospect of high speed connection from homes and businesses within the MAN to the academic institutions which also reside

there. Since the cable companies often already have cables installed to the home for other purposes, these developments offer opportunities for high speed, low cost connection to student homes and local schools in particular.

Asynchronous Transfer Mode (ATM)
The need to provide seamless voice, video and data services to the desktop requires the use of more advanced technologies. ATM is an emergent technology which will allow this seamless connectivity at high speed across both local and wide area networks. The cost of ATM switches and interface boards will gradually reduce to a level whereby use of ATM will become widespread, perhaps by the end of the decade.

Standards
Information which crosses the network must conform to standards which are common to the initiating and receiving stations. There are a number of de facto standards. These include:

• The X.400 standard supporting a store and forward message handling system to allow the network distribution of electronic text and graphics
• The X.500 standard allowing applications such as electronic mail to access directories, thus enabling global access to users
• World Wide Web, providing a standard for search and retrieval of text and graphics over the national and international networks (Internet).

Underlying standards are a number of protocols which define the structure of the data in transit. Common protocols include:

• The communications protocols, for example TCP/IP and IPX. TCP/IP is mainly used in a UNIX environment, while IPX is used in communication in a Novell Netware environment. Interworking between dissimilar protocols is often technically difficult
• The File Transfer Protocol (FTP), which facilitates the transmission of structured data files across a network.

Depending on the range of platforms and host systems in use, a range of standards and protocols or suitable alternatives need to be defined and supported by central IT services within an institution.

Platforms

Platforms cover the items of hardware and operating system software which may be required to support a learning environment. Logically they can be split into a number of categories:

Student workstations

Within a campus there should be a ready supply of workstations available for student use on a 24-hour, seven days per week basis. These should be networked and available in large clusters with adequate user support. Such clusters might be sited in strategic parts of the campus to allow students convenient access from their academic department or hall of residence.

Within a rich learning environment networked workstations might also be sited in student study bedrooms and in the home. The appropriate infrastructure will be required as indicated in the previous chapter.

The majority of workstations will be based on the IBM PC architecture; some will be Apple Macintosh systems and some will be more powerful workstations usually running the UNIX operating system or Open VMS.

Where multimedia applications are envisaged, the addition of CD-ROM drives and sound cards would also be required.

Staff workstations

Workstations for academic staff may be required for development purposes; the hardware should therefore be as fully configured as practical within institutional cost constraints. Developers should expect to have available the standard courseware authoring tools in use within an institution, as well as the software tools necessary to access appropriate financial and student data.

Servers

A server is a powerful networked computer which supports the filestore of a number of workstation users. Workstations communicate with the server using one of a number of standards, including PC-NFS for UNIX systems and Novell Netware for IBM PCs and Apple Macintoshes. Information can also be transferred between servers. Typical servers for a learning environment might include:

- A courseware server containing institutional courseware accessible from the student workstations
- A video-on-demand server containing video images of lectures and tutorials
- Library servers providing catalogue and book issue/return services
- Web servers providing information available to/from the World Wide Web
- MIS servers providing information on finance and student records
- General purpose servers providing access to commonly used software such as E-mail, spreadsheets and word processors.

All the servers need to observe the institutional guidelines on standards and protocols.

Other platforms

In order to support fully the learning environment the institution will also need to provide access to specialist facilities. These might include:

- Image capture – specialist cameras which can capture images to be used in courseware or on the World Wide Web

- Video recorders/televisions – available in public access areas to view hired institutional videos
- Video conferencing studios – available to allow interactive video conferencing between researchers or courseware developers
- CD-ROM mastering facilities
- Overhead and slide generation facilities.

What next?

This chapter has defined an architecture for the technical system which identifies eight major areas of information technology. Each area is composed of components which provide the services to support the roles at their workplaces.

The services to support the student are provided by the components from the application architecture. You should review the needs of the students in your learning environment, which you defined in chapter 8, and develop an application architecture to support this by following the example in this chapter.

The services to support the chunk and application developers are provided by the components from application development. You should review their needs and develop an architecture for application development following the example in this chapter.

The components you have now identified will themselves require services from the other areas. Review these needs and compare with the capabilities of your existing technical infrastructure components in order to build technical architectures for the remaining six areas.

The final chapter brings together the components of the architecture and shows how it can be used to manage change.

10

The Way Ahead

If you want to manage and control change to achieve optimum benefit, then you have already begun to manage change in your institution by reading this book, and you are probably wondering what to do next.

First, decide whether the ideas and approach are relevant to your institution, whether you want to adopt these and apply them, then decide how you are going to introduce them in your institution.

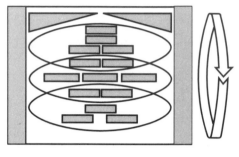

HEIs are moving into an era in which change will be one of the few constants, if not the only one. Those institutions who best understand how to control and manage change will be those best placed to prosper.

Creating an architecture for your own institution

Each HEI, and the individual faculties and departments within it, has a different starting point. Each will have different issues to address with varying priorities. Therefore there is not a single, preset solution appropriate to all institutions; each will need to create its own architecture, at the corporate level and for each faculty and department as appropriate, in line with the institution's own vision.

Before looking at the steps involved in how you might approach creating your own Learning Environment Architecture, it is probably useful to state that the process need not be viewed as strictly sequential . For example, in an ideal world you would probably start at the beginning, at the top, and work step by step through all the stages until you had created the 'brave new world' for your institution. However, we believe that this would be very impractical and almost certainly doomed to failure from the outset. Provided that you can define your business objectives clearly, but not necessarily at length, and you can establish a process for review and agreement, we recommend you start in the areas which will deliver the optimum return. Indeed a Learning Environment Architecture is itself a subset of an institution architecture.

Some HEIs will already have a vision statement and business objectives formally defined and documented in some form; others may not, but, as Gartner says, 'If business objectives are non-existent, create a proxy for them. This need not take a major effort, a back of an envelope approach will not be far off and can get the process started.'

We recommend that you apply the following steps to create a learning environment for your own institution.

Step 1

To create the right environment to develop an architecture you will need to:

- Appoint a senior manager as 'owner' of the architecture within the institution. That person will be responsible for developing the architecture and keeping it up to date
- Set up an architecture working group, comprising stakeholders from each part of the institution under the chairmanship of the 'owner'. You may consider inviting external stakeholders to participate in this
- Consider working with an external partner to guide and facilitate the architecture development and provide an independent view
- Define the objectives and scope of the architecture
- Produce a plan to resource, develop and review the progress of the architecture; get the plan underwritten by the appropriate senior manager or senior management team.

Step 2

As you proceed you will identify the need for a number of different tools to help you with different stages. There are a number which are offered by OPEN*framework* but none are prescribed. As an open system, to use the methodology, you can use whatever tools you choose; those that you prefer or just those that you know. It is probable that you will want to create a development/training plan covering the OPEN*framework* methodology and the tools you select, for those who will be directly involved.

Step 3

Review the components identified in this book, together with the issues specific to your institution.

In Chapter 2 we highlighted a number of trends and issues which we feel fairly certain will be pertinent to most HEIs; they will need to be acknowledged as HEIs develop architectures for themselves:

- Massification of education
- Competition and control
- Changing student profile
- The provision of learning resources.

To a greater or lesser extent all HEIs face the challenge of developing new and more appropriate learning environments for the twenty-first century and we believe that the method described in this architecture will help you to achieve this.

The first task that you need to carry out to create a comprehensive architecture is to establish the key business pressures facing your HEI. These may include the examples above, and will certainly extend beyond them. As the issues are documented, you can start on working out the implications at each of the business, social and technical system levels; you can apply your judgement to set some priorities for addressing these.

In Chapter 3 we considered managing change and discussed approaches to the following:

- Setting direction
- Evolving business strategy
- Business transformation.

Elsewhere in the book we have suggested that, in an ideal world, it would be nice to have the time, and other resources, to create an institution architecture by taking a holistic approach and applying the method from top to bottom, completing everything as you proceed. Creating an institution architecture is a bit like eating an elephant with a knife and fork. And how do you do that? Well cooked and in little chunks! As we said above, a learning environment architecture is in itself a subset of an institution architecture. The important thing again is to set the priorities for your institution, probably based on things like highest return for investment, ease of implementation/speed of return, no choice e.g. enforced by regulation, etc. In those areas you choose to pursue, don't miss out any of the steps. For example, it is essential that there is a direction-setting vision statement of some form, however brief, which can guide subsequent steps and ensuing decisions.

In Chapters 5 and 6 we looked at business objects and processes. You will need to tailor the definitions of the key business objects discussed to your own needs, and you should expect to add more detail to the models provided. It is likely that you will identify new business objects as you review and develop your business processes, or introduce new ones. For example, as you consider how you manage the interrelated development activities you will identify the need for planning documents and dependency controls.

Conversely, you can identify new processes by considering operations to be performed on the business objects. For example, operations on a learning chunk would include create, modify, withdraw, evaluate, etc. Each operation implies the need for a process.

Chapter 6 presented a business process model for the development, operation and continuous improvement of a learning environment for a generic institution. It identified and described a number of the key business processes in the top-level model.

Using a similar approach you need first to identify your business processes, then evaluate how well they match your current and future business requirements and decide what changes, if any, need to be made. The model presented here provides a useful reference point. We recommend that you use it to ensure completeness of your model. However, it is unlikely that you will wish to look at all your institution's processes at once. When you have determined what your key issues are, we recommend that you look at the processes relating to them.

You now need to capture for your HEI a picture of the external groups and bodies with which the HEI interfaces, the organisational structure (both current and targeted, if these are different), the roles people perform, and which workgroups are required. You must ensure that roles and workgroups are aligned to the business processes and the business needs.

Just as HEIs need to take focused decisions on their use of IT, so too they need to deploy their human resources strategically. This involves negotiating and agreeing the roles and responsibilities of different groups of staff, particularly academic and learning support staff. The process is likely to lead to changes from the current position. Staff in learning support centres, for example, are likely to take on increased responsibility for supporting student learning, and academics to specialise in one or more of the roles outlined in Chapter 7. Academic and learning support staff are likely to develop team skills as they jointly build the learning environment infrastructure, for example through the development and adaptation of materials and software for student learning.

Chapter 8 covered the topics of workplaces and services, and we described particularly the workplaces and services for the student. You now need to write down for each role identified in your social system the workplaces and services required. Then, using the OPEN*framework* qualities, define the workplace requirements. You can use the detailed example provided for the student role to help you do this. This will result in a more complete workplace model. It is likely that you will also extend the service provision mechanisms model.

You also need to build a learnplace table for your institution. How you do this was described in identifying and aggregating learnplaces in Chapter 8.

You will have now identified a detailed set of service requirements for your institution's learning environment. These are grouped together into components in the application layer of the technical architecture which we described in Chapter 9. This chapter has defined an architecture for the technical system which identifies eight major areas of information technology. Each area is composed of components which provide the services to support the roles at their workplaces.

The services to support the student are provided by the components from the application architecture. You should review the needs of the students in your learning environment, which you defined in Chapter 8, and develop an application architecture to support this by following the example in Chapter 9.

The services to support the chunk and application developers are provided by the components from application development. You should review their needs and develop an architecture for application development following the example in this chapter.

The components you have now identified will themselves require services from the other areas. Review these needs and compare with the capabilities of your existing technical infrastructure components in order to build technical architectures for the remaining six areas.

In working our way through the chapters, as we have just done, you will have noticed we have bypassed Chapter 4 which discussed perspectives and qualities. This is to make the point that we recommend that you do consider all elements of the architecture from the seven perspectives:

- Enterprise manager
- Student
- Employee
- Trading partner
- User
- Service provider
- Developer

and the five qualities:

- availability, usability, performance, security and potential for change.

Step 4

Document the architecture and get it approved. It then needs to be communicated to the appropriate people both inside and outside the institution. The next step is to use it to identify which changes are to be implemented. Careful planning is needed for each change. Key features of any plan must be evolution and the protection of existing assets which will be required to continue to provide services during the transition, and may offer additional scope for exploitation.

and finally . . .

The Learning Environment Architecture methodology described in this book makes no claims to be definitive, and does not prescribe the use of any particular management tools. It has been developed in order to help any HEI which wants to develop its own architecture, by providing a method which can be expanded or adapted to meet the specific needs of that institution; it seeks to illustrate the applicability of OPENframework as a practical means of dealing with the issues confronting HEIs in the mid-1990s.

The Learning Environment Architecture is supplier-independent and specifically tailored for use by HEIs.

If you want to manage change, rather than be managed by it, the Learning Environment Architecture provides a method which can be used by your institution.

Appendix A: Bibliography

Teaching and learning in higher education

Coffield, F. (ed.) (1995) *Higher Education in a Learning Society*. Durham: University of Durham.

Committee of Scottish University Principals (1992) *Teaching and Learning in an Expanding Higher Education System* [The MacFarlane Report]. Edinburgh: SCFC.

Committee of Vice Chancellors and Principals of the Universities of the United Kingdom [CVCP] (1985) *Report of the Steering Committee for Efficiency Studies in Universities* [The Jarratt Report]. London: CVCP.

Computers in Teaching Initiative (1992) *Computers in University Teaching: Core Tools for Core Activities*. Oxford: CTISS Publications.

Computers in Teaching Initiative (1994) *Higher Education 1998 Transformed by Learning Technology*. Oxford: CTISS Publications.

de Jong, T. and Sarti, L. (eds) (1994) *Design and Production of Multimedia and Simulation-based Learning Material*. Dordrecht: Kluwer.

European Commission (1993) *Negotiating European Competence Representation and Recognition*, a Delta Project outline. Nectar occasional paper NL/5/93. Brussels: EC.

Freeman, R. and Lewis, R. (1995) *Writing Open Learning Materials*. Lancaster: Framework Press.

Hague, D. (1991) *Beyond Universities: a New Republic of the Intellect*. London: Institute of Economic Affairs.

Honey, P. and Mumford, A. (1992) *The Manual of Learning Styles*. Maidenhead: P. Honey.

Joint Information Systems Committee [JISC] (1995a) *Exploiting Information Systems in Higher Education: an Issues Paper*. Bristol: JISC.

Joint Information Systems Committee (1995b) *Guidelines for Developing an Information Strategy*, a report from the Information Strategy Steering Group. Bristol: JISC.

Laurillard, D. (1993) *Rethinking University Teaching*. London: Routledge.

Race, P. (1994) *The Open Learning Handbook*. London: Kogan Page.

Shuell, T. (1992) Designing instructional computer systems for meaningful learning, in M. Jones and P. Winne (eds) *Adaptive Learning Environments*. New York: Springer Verlag.

R. J. S. Stokes (1994) *Computer Assisted Learning in Engineering at the University of Humberside*. London: Open Learning Foundation.

Tennyson, R. and Barron, A. (eds) (1994) *Automating Instructional Design: Computer-based Development and Delivery Tools – Automating Instructional Design*. Berlin: Springer Verlag.

University Funding Council Information Systems Committee (1992) *Beyond Lectures*, a report from the Information Systems Committee Courseware Development Working Party. Oxford: CTISS Publications.

Van den Brande, L. (1993) *Flexible and Distance Learning*. Chichester: Wiley.

Other papers

Cochinaux, P. and de Woot, P. (1995) *Moving towards the Learning Society*, a white paper on education and training. Brussels: The Association of European Universities and the European Round Table.

European Commission (1994) *Europe and the Global Information Society* [The Bangemann Report]. Brussels: EC.

Further Education Funding Council (1996) *Report of the Learning and Technology Committee* [The Higginson Report]. Coventry: FEFC.

Management

Brown, G. (1994) *Capturing Vision*. Bracknell: ICL Enterprise Technology.

Gale, A. (1994) *Evolving Business Strategy*. Bracknell: ICL Enterprise Technology.

Hammer, M. and Champy, J. (1993) *Re-engineering the Corporation: a Manifesto for Business Revolution*. New York: HarperCollins.

Handy, C. (1989) *The Age of Unreason*. Boston, Mass.: Harvard Business School Publishing.

ICL (1993) Various articles on OPENframework, *ICL Technical Journal*, May.

Massachusetts Institute of Technology, Sloan School of Management [MIT/Sloan] (1990) *Management in the 1990s Research Program: Final Report*. Boston, Mass.: MIT.

National Council for Education Technology (1995) *Managing IT: a Planning Tool for Managers*. Coventry: NCET.

Scott-Morton, M. S. (ed.) (1991) *The Corporation of the 1990s*. Oxford: Oxford University Press.

Thurlby, R. (1995) *An Overview of Strategic Alignment*. Slough: ICL.

Other books in the OPEN*framework* series

Most of the following books are published by Prentice Hall in Cambridge and cover the qualities, elements and specialisations of OPEN*framework* in much more detail. The more recent titles, those marked with an asterisk, are only available on the CD-ROM *Architext*, published by ICL, which contains all the books.

General

Overview of Methods*
Brunt, R. and Hutt, A. T. F. (1992) *The Systems Architecture: an Introduction. Transforming your Business with IT**

Qualities

Smethurst, R. (1993) *Availability.*
Sutcliffe, S. (1993) *Performance.*
Pratten, G. (1993) *Potential for Change.*
Fairthorne, B. (1993) *Security.*
Hutt, A. T. F. (1993) *Usabililty.*

Elements

Brenner, J. (1993) *Distributed Application Services.*
Brown, G. H. (1993) *Application Development.*
Deignan, F. D. (1993) *Networking Services.*
Gale, A. C. (1993) *Systems Management.*
Hutt, A. T. F. (1993) *User Interface.*
Kay, M. H. (1993) *Information Management.*
McVitie, D. (1993) *Platforms.*

Specialisations

Lucas R. (1993) *Services.*
Sutcliffe, S. (1994) *Local Government Architecture: a Method for Managing Change.*
CALS*
Client Server*
Manufacturing*
Office Applications*
Retail Banking Applications*

Appendix B: Glossary

Application
Software which exploits information technology to support the business processes of an organisation.

Application model
A representation of an application which facilitates discussion of its attributes.

Architecture
In this book, an architecture is defined as a framework aligning the needs of the business, its people and the capabilities of technology which recognises that they are all continuously changing. It is a tool which provides a structure for managing this change and a set of standards, conventions and rules which support the effective integration of business, social and technical systems.

Asset model
An asset model describes the assets of an organisation, identifying which are vital to the business, defined as core assets, which will require to be protected and developed, and those which are less vital or non-core, which could be sold off and services outsourced as required.

Availability
Availability is one of the five OPEN*framework* qualities and is a measure of whether a system is there when it is needed, and whether it delivers the defined service to the agreed service.

Business object
A business object is a building block that is used by any of the people in the social system. There are two types of business object: an *elemental* business object is the lowest level of object. An example of an elemental business object is a book used by the student role in the learning process; an *aggregated* business object is a higher level of object which contains lower level objects. An example of an aggregated business object is a learning environment.

Business process
A defined set of tasks and responsibilities, carried out by people or systems, that can be used repeatedly, and can be directly related to the objectives of the business.

CAL
Computer-assisted learning

CATS
Credit accumulation and transfer systems – the system whereby students are credited with achievement points for the successful completion of modules or other units of learning to predefined standards. The student can then move on to study other modules or units, at the same or different learning institutions, which will take account of the previous points earned. These points can thus be accumulated and contribute to the final award of a degree.

CBL
Computer-based learning

Core assets
A core asset is one that is deemed to be critical to the successful achievement of an enterprise's business strategy.

Critical success factors
Critical success factors are activities or events identified in a plan which must take effect, usually in the planned timescale, in order for the plan to succeed. They can be used as measures to determine whether or not objectives have been successfully achieved.

CTI
The Computers in Teaching Initiative is a UK-wide programme which supports and encourages the development and exploitation of learning environments which use information and communication technologies.

CVCP
Committee of Vice-Chancellors and Principals

ECTS
The European Credit Transfer System is an experimental system intended to allow employers and universities in one EU country to interpret and recognise qualifications obtained in another.

Elements
The OPEN*framework* elements describe the parts of an architecture.

Enterprise
An organisation independent enough to decide its own strategy, for example a higher education institution.

Enterprise manager
A member of the executive management team of an enterprise.

HEI
Higher education institution

HTML
HyperText Markup Language (HTML) is the computer language that is used to mark up documents to enable hypertext links to be followed, thus linking documents over a computer network.

Hyperlink
The link made between documents held on a network via HTML.

Hypertext
Computer-based text that contains pointers to other related text elsewhere in a network, which could be accessed, for example through the Internet, and held anywhere in the world.

ICT
Information and communications technology

Information meta-model
An information meta-model defines the rules by which information is structured and accessed. Associated with a meta-model is an application programming interface or data manipulation language reflecting the operations defined by the meta-model.

Information strategy
A strategic plan to exploit information resources in the broadest sense throughout an enterprise. An information strategy needs to start from, and encapsulate, the vision of the enterprise, and will often be part of a hierarchy of strategies under the enterprise business strategy. An information strategy may include, *but is not*, either an information systems strategy and/or an information technology strategy.

Information superhighway
A set of computer networks of a national and international scale which are very widely available, especially to the public, and containing a wealth of information. The Internet is widely recognised as the prototype of an information superhighway.

Information system
The collection of applications, infrastructure, trained people and processes working together within an organisation to process, record, and communicate information.

Information technology (IT)
Computers and associated technology, used as part of an information system.

Internet
A group of world-wide networks, using a common protocol (IP, the Internet Protocol) such that data can be transmitted seamlessly. There are many thousands of computers acting as servers for the networks, estimated at 25,000 at the beginning of 1995, but growth appears to be exponential; there are many millions of users. As well as a huge wealth of information, the Internet supports a number of facilities such as electronic mail and the World Wide Web (or the Web, see below). The Internet can be accessed via JANET (see below) or via a variety of Internet service providers (or ISPs), who charge a fee for their services. Otherwise much of the information accessible on the Internet is made freely available although, increasingly, information provided is being charged for. More and more commercial transactions are daily taking place on the Internet, usually through the Web.

JANET/SuperJANET
The Joint Academic Network is the implementation of a high speed communications network which interconnects all subscribing HEIs, research council sites, and other bodies with a legitimate interest in higher education in the UK. SuperJANET is the even higher speed implementation of JANET which is now offered as an option to JANET. JANET and SuperJANET connect with the Internet.

JISC
Joint Information Systems Committee

Learning chunk
A learning chunk is a bounded learning activity including, at a minimum level, a specified set of learning objectives and a set of assessment procedures capable of testing to what extent these outcomes are met by students. A learning chunk may contain other elements. A detailed description of a learning chunk is given in the section starting on page 57.

Learning environment
A learning environment is a community with its own culture and values providing a variety of learnplaces that support student learning.

Learning function
The student learning process may be split into a number of subprocesses called learning functions. The number and definition of these functions vary according to the level of decomposition taken in the approach. Learning functions should be mutually independent but taken together should cover all parts of student learning. Examples of different ways of approaching the decomposition of the student learning process into learning functions are shown in Appendix C.

Learning method
A learning method is an activity in which a student participates in order to complete the learning process. Learning methods include the lecture, the tutorial, the seminar, practical work, assessment and individual study, among others.

Learning resource
A learning resource is any resource used to support student learning including books, guidance from academic staff, CAL systems, laboratory equipment and so on.

Learning vehicle
A set of learning resources designed to enable students to meet the objectives of a learning chunk. A learning chunk will include only one learning vehicle which may include a number of complementary learntasks, learnplaces, and learning resource lists.

Learnplace
A learnplace is a student workplace equipped to support one or more learning methods.

Learntask
A learntask is a student learning activity.

Multimedia
The capture and presentation of information that combines diverse information types and different content formats including for example, motion video, audio, still images, graphics, animation and character text.

NCET
National Council for Educational Technology

NCVQ
National Council for Vocational Qualifications

NECTAR
Negotiating European Competence Representation and Recognition – an EU-funded project in the DELTA programme which was concerned with

methods of analysing and representing competences. The NECTAR project gave a central place to Pierre Levy's *arbre de connaissances* approach to representing competences.

Networking
Technology that allows platforms (see below) to be interconnected and applications to interwork.

NVQ
National Vocational Qualification

Object orientation
A set of computing principles that group together real-world objects and the processing associated with them to provide components that can be reused and distributed.

OLF
Open Learning Foundation

OPEN*framework*
OPEN*framework* is a method for managing change which aligns the systems of an enterprise using the principles of architecture.

Performance
Performance is one of the five OPEN*framework* qualities and is a measure of the rate at which a system is able to perform useful work and the responsiveness with which the results are presented.

Perspectives
The requirements of an element in the architecture expressed from the viewpoints of the different people, both inside and outside the institution, who will come into contact with it and who will have different needs, for example student, staff, manager, trading partner.

Platform
A collection of hardware and software components with the ability to process and store information.

Potential for change
Potential for change is one of the five OPEN*framework* qualities and is a measure of a system's ability, in the future, to retain or increase its value to the institution.

Process
A defined set of tasks and responsibilities, carried out by people or systems, that can be used repeatedly.

Process model
A formal description of a process.

Process re-engineering
A fundamental redesign of business processes.

Qualities
These define criteria for each of the elements of the architecture to ensure that an institution's systems meet its requirements. OPEN*framework* defines five qualities: availability, usability, performance, security and potential for change.

Security
Security is one of the five OPEN*framework* qualities and is a measure of a system's ability to respond to a threat.

SEDA
Staff and Educational Development Association

Service level agreement
An agreement between the commissioner and provider of services which defines the level of performance to be provided.

Social system
The social system includes all aspects of how users think and behave, how they work together in groups, and the material things that support them. Describing the social system helps an enterprise to relate desired changes to its whole business activities, rather than describing them in terms of technology alone.

SuperJANET
see JANET above

Technical strategy
The technical strategy defines the information systems that an enterprise needs to implement its vision.

TLTP
The Teaching and Learning Technology Programme funds the development of reusable technology-based learning resources and encourages their incorporation into learning chunks.

Trading partner
A third-party organisation or individual that has a relationship with the enterprise. Such relationships may have either a direct or indirect influence on the performance of the enterprise and require to be managed. Some examples of trading partners are discussed on page 40.

UCoSDA
Universities and Colleges Staff Development Agency

Usability
Usability is one of the five OPEN*framework* qualities and is a measure of whether customers or users are able to carry out specific tasks effectively, efficiently and with satisfaction.

Value chain
A linked set of value-creating activities, going from the supply of raw materials through to the ultimate delivery of the end product to consumers.

Video on demand (VoD)
A service which can store large numbers of video-based materials on a central server and deliver selected video titles, on demand, to users connected online over a communications network.

Vision
A vision is a description of something an enterprise would like to create (e.g. an organisation, a business activity, a corporate culture). A vision should provide direction for the enterprise and sustain and motivate the people within it.

WWW or World Wide Web (W3 or the Web)
This is a public domain distributed multimedia information system. Developed by CERN Information, it can be accessed by referring to 'pages' of information usually held on servers in the Internet (see above). Related information can be accessed by selecting highlighted words, or pictures, on the page. Resources are provided in a standardised way and can be linked indefinitely, thus providing a truly world-wide information system.

Workgroup
A group of people within an enterprise interacting with each other to achieve a common goal.

Workplace
A workplace is the formalisation of the user interface, embracing the working environment and the hardware and software used to deliver the user interface. It also includes the applications and the services, training and documentation provided to users. A learnplace is the specialisation of the student workplace in the learning environment.

Appendix C: Learning Functions

In this book we subscribe to a view of learning which is labelled guided construction in Table C.1.

We can better understand and hence improve the student learning process if we divide it into smaller subprocesses. This can be done in a variety of ways. We offer three further such decompositions in this appendix. The first (Table C.2) was derived from Tom Shuell's learning functions model (1992). It may be used to assess the completeness and internal cohesion of learning packages.

Table C.1 Ways of conceptualising the learning process

View of learning	Description
Passive reception	Implies a view of knowledge as something that can be broken into discrete pieces and passed intact from a teacher to a learner. It is usually accompanied by a view of the learner as inactive – an empty vessel to be filled
Discovery	Argues that knowledge cannot be predigested and passed from one mind to another. Rather, the learner must work hard at interpreting what they experience, building their own unique understandings through voyages of personal discovery. Since it is difficult for a teacher (or any 'outsider') to know what will best fuel a learner's personal sense-making, the discovery approach tends to frown on intervention, leaving the learner free to plot their own course.
Guided construction	Gives the learner a very active part in their own learning; the learner constructs their own knowledge in a way which resembles the discovery approach. However, it also gives an important role to external guidance, whether from a teacher, a computer program or other learners.

Table C.2 Twelve subprocesses of student learning

Learning function	Description
Expectation	Important for the learner to have an idea of what they are trying to accomplish. But (in Guided construction) this does not always imply explicit setting of instructional objectives at start of activity; rather expectations may evolve and clarify throughout a learning episode
Motivation	The learner's willingness to contribute effort and persist in the task
Prior-knowledge activation	New knowledge builds on old; the learner needs to retrieve relevant knowledge from long-term memory
Attention	Multiplicity of information coming at the learner; he or she needs to attend to that information which is relevant to the current learning task and ignore the rest
Encoding	Find ways of encoding new information so that it integrates with existing knowledge and can be retrieved when required
Comparison	A part of 'sense-making' work involved in meaningful learning; learning new facts, concepts, etc.; trying to establish similarities, differences, etc.
Hypothesis generation	Meaningful learning requires the learner to generate various hypotheses as they seek an understanding of the new material: 'Does this mean x?', 'Is y the case?'
Repetition	A single exposure is rarely enough to make sense of any complex information. Intelligently varying repetition, rather than rote, is an important aid to learning
Feedback	For example, as a consequence of hypothesis making – 'Am I on the right track?'
Evaluation	Receiving feedback is not enough, the learner must evaluate the feedback; does it make sense?
Monitoring	Engagement of self-regulatory processes: 'What do I know and what do I still need to know?' 'How am I getting on?' 'Should I change tack?'
Combination, integration, synthesis	Pulling the pieces together; combining fragments of new information into meaningful wholes; making connections; restructuring

Tutor initiated	*Learner initiated*
For example, provide overview (map, diagram), statement of purpose	Identify purpose of learning activity
Opportunities for interaction; interesting materials	Look for ways to make personally relevant or enjoyable
Remind learner of related/ prerequisite information	Ask self what is already known about the topic
For example, use of highlights, animation, audio in CAL programs, stressing key points in lectures	Identify key features, record notes
Suggest mnemonics, provide diagrams or multiple examples	Generate mnemonics, images, examples, contexts for application
Encourage through use of diagrams, charts, questions	Look for similarities
Encourage learner to think of, and try, alternative courses of action	Generate possible alternatives and corresponding solutions
Guided practice and guided reflection, multiple perspectives and examples	Systematic reviews
Provide instructionally relevant, timely feedback	Seek answers to self-posed questions
Organise things so that the next action of learner is based on evaluation of feedback received	Ask 'What do I currently know now?', 'What do I need to know?'
Check for understanding	Monitor performance; self-test
Provide ways to combine/integrate information	Establish categories, construct tables, seek higher-order relationships

Table C.3 Six functions of student learning (based on Committee of Scottish University Principals 1992).

Learning function	Description
Orientation	At the start of a learning event, the student needs to understand and accept the aims and methods involved in the event and to bring relevant prior knowledge to bear. During the event they need to monitor and/or respond to monitoring information about their progress
Motivation	A negotiation (which may be wholly internal to the student's mind) has to take place, which seeks to align the aims and methods of the learning event with the goals and preferences of the student. This may recur during the learning event
Information acquisition	The student attends to the information (made) available during the learning event and encodes representations of it into long-term memory
Elaboration	The student elaborates the representations of what they have just learned, especially by making further connections with what they already know and by building additional higher-order representations (for example, more abstract schemata)
Clarification	In the process of creating and elaborating representations, the student acts to resolve ambiguities/uncertainties . . .
Confirmation	And obtains information intended for this purpose

Table C.4 is based on extensive, if informal, field research carried out by Professor Phil Race and reported in *The Open Learning Handbook* (Race 1994). It draws on other research such as that of Donald Kolb. Analysing the responses of hundreds of learners, collected in workshops, Race identified the activities set out (in slightly adapted form) in Table C.4.

Table C.4 Four functions of student learning

Learning function	Description
Motivation	The impetus or 'want' to learn
Practice	Learner activity in whatever form: for example, asking or answering questions, writing essays or reports, playing music, acting, undertaking experiments, going on a work placement, manipulating a program
Feedback	Responses to the learner's activity: for example, via tutor, peers, computer; provision of formal or informal assessment information
Reflection	Making sense of activity carried out at the 'practice' stage, and the feedback on it. Reflection can include extracting fundamental principles, designing a different approach to a task, revising one's study methods

Index

The Society for Research into Higher Education

The Society for Research into Higher Education exists to stimulate and coordinate research into all aspects of higher education. It aims to improve the quality of higher education through the encouragement of debate and publication on issues of policy, on the organization and management of higher education institutions, and on the curriculum and teaching methods.

The Society's income is derived from subscriptions, sales of its books and journals, conference fees and grants. It receives no subsidies, and is wholly independent. Its individual members include teachers, researchers, managers and students. Its corporate members are institutions of higher education, research institutes, professional, industrial and governmental bodies. Members are not only from the UK, but from elsewhere in Europe, from America, Canada and Australasia, and it regards its international work as among its most important activities.

Under the imprint *SRHE & Open University Press*, the Society is a specialist publisher of research, having some 60 titles in print. The Editorial Board of the Society's Imprint seeks authoritative research or study in the above fields. It offers competitive royalties, a highly recognizable format in both hardback and paperback and the world-wide reputation of the Open University Press.

The Society also publishes *Studies in Higher Education* (three times a year), which is mainly concerned with academic issues, *Higher Education Quarterly* (formerly *Universities Quarterly*), mainly concerned with policy issues, *Research into Higher Education Abstracts* (three times a year), and *SRHE News* (four times a year).

The Society holds a major annual conference in December, jointly with an institution of higher education. In 1993, the topic was 'Governments and the Higher Education Curriculum: Evolving Partnerships' at the University of Sussex in Brighton. In 1994, it was 'The Student Experience' at the University of York and in 1995, 'The Changing University' at Heriot-Watt University in Edinburgh. Conferences in 1996 include 'Working in Higher Education' at Cardiff Institute of Higher Education.

The Society's committees, study groups and branches are run by the members. The groups at present include:

Teacher Education Study Group
Continuing Education Group
Staff Development Group
Excellence in Teaching and Learning

Benefits to members

Individual

Individual members receive:

- *SRHE News*, the Society's publications list, conference details and other material included in mailings.
- Greatly reduced rates for *Studies in Higher Education* and *Higher Education Quarterly*.
- A 35 per cent discount on all SRHE & Open University Press publications.
- Free copies of the Proceedings – commissioned papers on the theme of the Annual Conference.
- Free copies of *Research into Higher Education Abstracts*.
- Reduced rates for conferences.
- Extensive contacts and scope for facilitating initiatives.
- Reduced reciprocal memberships.
- Free copies of the *Register of Members' Research Interests*.

Corporate

Corporate members receive:

- All benefits of individual members, plus
- Free copies of *Studies in Higher Education*.
- Unlimited copies of the Society's publications at reduced rates.
- Special rates for its members e.g. to the Annual Conference.
- The right to submit application for the Society's research grants.

 Membership details: SRHE, 3 Devonshire Street, London WIN 2BA, UK. Tel: 0171 637 2766. Fax: 0171 637 2781
Catalogue: SRHE & Open University Press, Celtic Court, 22 Ballmoor, Buckingham MK18 1XW. Tel: (01280) 823388.